R. W. SCHAMBACH
PRESENTS

The Price of God's Miracle-Working Power

Contents

A. A. Allen
1911 - 1970

This powerful faith classic was written by Evangelist A. A. Allen some four decades ago, but has been out of circulation in recent years. Because I consider it one of the most important Christian books ever produced, I am happy to be able to present it anew to a new generation of readers who need its biblical message now more than ever.

A. A. Allen was one of the most important evangelists to emerge in the early days of the healing revival. From the beginning he was a prophet to the poor. He related to their feelings and needs in a way few public figures do, and demonstrated great compassion for them.

His great tent crusades reached masses of people across America, as did his TV and radio outreaches, and his books and literature.

I had the privilege of serving as Brother Allen's associate evangelist for six years during the 1950s. I learned so much about faith and the miraculous from this man of God, with whom I ministered with deep admiration and respect.

I pray this book will encourage, inspire, and bless you as it has so many others over the years.

And by it he being dead yet speaketh (Hebrews 11:4).

R. W. Schambach

Chapter 1

THE PRICE OF GOD'S MIRACLE-WORKING POWER

How long had I been here in this closet? Days ...or just hours? It seemed like days since, at my own request, I had heard my wife lock that closet door from the outside! What would she think about me shutting myself away for so long? Had it really been days, or just hours? Was I really getting anywhere with God? Would God answer? Would He satisfy that hunger in my soul, or would I have to admit defeat again as I had done so many times before? No! I'd stay right here on my knees until God answered, or I would die in the attempt! Hadn't God's Word said, *They that wait upon the Lord shall renew their strength; they shall mount up with wings as eagles; they shall run, and not be weary* (Isaiah 40:31)?

Had my wife opened the door? No, it was still closed! But the light—where was the light coming from? Then I began to realize that the light filling my prayer closet was God's glory! It wasn't the closet door that had opened, but the door of heaven!

The presence of God was so real and powerful that I felt I would die right there on my knees. It seemed that if God came any closer, I could not stand it! Yet I wanted it and was determined to have it. Little wonder that Paul, under like circumstances, *fell to the earth* (Acts 9:4). No wonder John *fell at his feet as dead* (Revelation 1:17).

Was this my answer? Was God going to speak to me? Would God satisfy my longing heart at last, after these many years? I seemed to lose consciousness of everything except the mighty presence of God. I trembled...I tried to see Him and then was afraid that I would, for suddenly I realized that should I see Him, I would die (see Exodus 33:20). Just His glorious presence was enough!

Then like a whirlwind, I heard His voice. It was God! He was speaking to me! This was the glorious answer I had sought so diligently and had been waiting for since my conversion at the age of twenty-three. This was what my longing soul had cried for ever since God called me into the ministry.

That call had come with such force and was so definite, that nothing could ever make me doubt it was of God. Even though my past life had not properly prepared me for ministry, I knew God was calling me.

From the time of my conversion, I realized my need of concentrated study if I was to effectively fulfill the call of God upon my life. I spent many hours reading the Bible and seeking to understand its message and meaning. To my simple, untaught soul, God seemed to mean exactly what He said—and He seemed to be saying it directly to me through His Word: *As ye go, preach, saying, The kingdom of heaven is at hand. HEAL THE SICK, cleanse the lepers, raise the dead, cast out devils: freely ye have received, freely give* (Matthew 10:7,8). All this seemed to be included in a call to the ministry, yet I did not see it being done! I myself was powerless to carry out these commands of Christ. Yet I knew that it could be done, for Christ would not give a command that could not be carried out!

Before my conversion, I knew so little about God and His Word, that I couldn't even quote John 3:16 or name the four Gospels. In the Methodist church where I was converted, I was not taught to seek the baptism with the Holy Ghost such as the disciples received on the Day of Pentecost. Nor was I taught to expect the signs mentioned in Mark 16:17,18 to follow me as a believer in the Lord. I was taught to believe on the Lord Jesus Christ for salvation. And I was gloriously saved and set free from condemnation of sin. Then, as I searched the Scriptures, I asked God to direct me to the portions that would be the most beneficial to me. The Lord began to reveal to me the truths of the baptism of the Holy Ghost, the signs following, the gifts of the Spirit, and the supernatural things of God.

It was not long until God led me into a Pentecostal church. There I began to see the blessings of God and some of the manifestations of the Spirit. It was in these meetings that I became convinced of my need for the baptism with the Holy Spirit. I began to pray and earnestly seek God for that experience.

Thirty days after my conversion, while attending a camp meeting in Miami, Oklahoma I was gloriously filled with the Holy Ghost and spoke in other tongues as the Spirit gave utterance.

I had read, *Ye shall receive power, after that the Holy Ghost is come upon you* (Acts 1:8), so I fully expected that I would immediately have power to heal the sick and perform miracles. But it didn't take me long to realize that more was required than the baptism with the Holy Ghost, in order to consistently see these results. The baptism with the Spirit provides access to this power, but the gifts of the Spirit provide the channels for its operation. I immediately began to pray and seek the gifts of the Spirit. I felt I must have power to heal the sick, for I knew that God never called anyone to preach the gospel without also commissioning him to heal the sick.

The power of the Holy Ghost may be likened to the power of electricity. When one is filled with the Spirit, it is like wiring a building, and establishing connection with the "power house." Many people use electricity for years just to provide light— never taking advantage of the conveniences that are available through using the various appliances powered by electricity. The gifts of the Spirit may be likened to these appliances. As new gifts are added, more work can be done with greater ease. The power does not change, but it is made more effective. God never intended for His people to stop after being filled with the Spirit. It is just the beginning. We are told to *covet earnestly the best gifts* (1 Corinthians 12:31). This is the path to greater accomplishments for God.

Two years after my conversion, I married and began my ministry. For more than a year, my wife and I continued preaching the glorious gospel of salvation, the baptism with the Spirit, the second coming of Christ, and divine healing. In every revival meeting I always scheduled at least two nights each week to preach divine healing and pray for the sick. During this time, we saw a large number of miraculous healings as God honored the preaching of His Word. But I knew that God's plan included greater things for me and I believed there would come a time when this plan would be a reality in my life.

Many times my wife and I searched the Scriptures together. Each time we became more convinced that God's promises concerning the gifts of the Spirit, the signs following, healings, and miracles were meant for us today. It was also clear that we did not possess this power in the fullness God had promised. We knew there must be a scriptural reason why we were lacking this power. Since God cannot lie, the fault had to be within us!

11

While pastoring my first church, in Colorado, I made up my mind that I had to hear from heaven and know the reason why my ministry was not confirmed by signs and wonders. I felt sure that if I fasted and prayed, God would reveal what stood between me and His miracle-working power in my ministry. I was so hungry for the power of God in my life that I felt I could not stand in my pulpit and preach again, until I heard from Him. I told my wife of my plan to wait on God for the answer.

It was then that I had the greatest battle of my life. Satan was determined that I should not fast and pray until God answered. Many times he whipped me by tricking me out of that prayer closet. Satan knew that if I ever actually contacted God it would hinder his evil cause. So he set out to do all in his power to keep me from making that contact.

Day after day I went into the prayer closet, determined to stay until God spoke to me. Again and again I came out without the answer.

Again and again my wife would say to me, "I thought you said this was the time you were going to stay until you got the answer." Then she would smile in her own sweet way, remembering that *the spirit indeed is willing, but the flesh is weak* (Matthew 26:41).

Again and again I answered her, "Honey, I really meant to pray it through this time, but—!" It seemed there was always a reason why I couldn't stay in that closet until the answer came. I always justified myself by saying I would pray it through tomorrow. Things would be more favorable then.

The Lord encouraged my heart by calling to my attention how Daniel held on in fasting and prayer. He wrested the answer from the hands of Satan, even though it took three weeks to do so (see Daniel 10:1,12).

So the next day I was on my knees in the closet again. I had told my wife I would never come out until I heard from God, and I really thought I meant it.

But a few hours later, as I noticed the aroma of food being prepared, I was out of the closet and in the kitchen, inquiring, "What smells so delicious, dear?"

At the table a few moments later, God spoke to my heart. I had only taken one bite of food, but I stopped. God had spoken to me. I knew in that moment that until I wanted to hear from God more than anything else in the world—more than food and gratification of the flesh—I would never get my answer from God.

I quickly arose from the table and said to my wife, "Honey, I mean business with God this time! I'm going back into the closet, and I want you to lock me inside. I am going to stay there until I hear from God." I had said this so many times before that she was beginning to wonder if I really could subdue the flesh long enough to defeat the devil.

"Oh," she replied, "you'll be knocking for me to open the door in an hour or so." Nevertheless, I heard her lock the door from the outside, saying "I'll let you out any time you knock."

I answered, "I'll not knock until I have the answer that I have wanted so long." At last I had definitely made up my mind to stay there until I heard from God—no matter what the cost!

Hour after hour I battled the devil and the flesh in that closet! Many times I almost gave up. It seemed to me that days were slipping by, and my progress was so slow! Many times I was tempted to give it all up and try to be satisfied without the answer—to just go on as I had been doing. But deep in my soul I knew I could never be satisfied doing that. I had tried it and found that it was not enough. So I kept on waiting.

And now something was happening!

I don't know how long I had been in the closet when this happened, and it doesn't matter. I just know I prayed until it happened!

The presence of God was so real...so wonderful ...and so powerful! In His presence, I felt like one of the small pebbles at the foot of the towering Rockies. I felt unworthy to even hear His voice. But He wasn't speaking to me because I was worthy, He was speaking because I was needy. Centuries ago He had promised to supply that need, and this was the fulfillment of that promise.

It seemed that God was talking to me faster

than any human could possibly speak—and faster than I could follow, mentally. My heart cried out, "Speak a little more slowly. I want to remember it all!" Yet I knew I could never forget! God was giving me a list of the things which stood between me and His power. After each new requirement was added to the list in my mind, there followed a brief explanation about the requirement and its importance.

If I had known there were so many things to remember, I would have brought a pencil and paper! I hadn't expected God to speak in such a definite way, giving me such a long list. I never dreamed I was falling so far short of the glory of God. I hadn't realized there were so many things in my life that generated doubt and hindered my faith.

As God continued to speak to me, I began to feel in my pockets for a pencil. At last I located one and began searching for a piece of paper. I couldn't find any. Suddenly I remembered the cardboard box filled with winter clothes that I was using for an altar. I would write on the box.

Now I was ready!

I asked the Lord to please start all over again at the beginning and let me write the things down, one at a time. I asked Him to speak slowly so I could get it down on paper.

Once more, God started at the beginning and repeated the many things He had already revealed to me. As God spoke to me, I wrote down what He said.

When the last requirement was written down on the list, God spoke once again. He said, "This is the answer. When you have placed on the altar of consecration and obedience the last thing on your list, YE SHALL NOT ONLY HEAL THE SICK, BUT IN MY NAME SHALL YE CAST OUT DEVILS. YE SHALL SEE MIGHTY MIRACLES AS, IN MY NAME, YE PREACH THE WORD. FOR BEHOLD, I GIVE YOU POWER OVER ALL THE POWER OF THE ENEMY."

God then revealed to me the things that were hindrances to my ministry—the things that prevented Him from working with me, confirming the Word with signs following. They were the very same things which were hindering thousands of others.

Now it began to grow darker in the closet. I felt His mighty power begin to lift. For a few more moments His presence lingered...and then I was alone. Alone, yet not alone.

I trembled under the mighty lingering presence of God. In the dark, I fumbled at the bottom of the cardboard box, tearing off the list I had written down. At last, here was the price I must pay in order to have the power of God in my life and ministry—the price tag for the MIRACLE-WORKING POWER OF GOD!

Frantically, I pounded on the locked door. Again

and again I pounded. At last, I heard my wife coming. She opened the door and the moment she saw me, she knew I had been with God. Her first words were, "You've got the answer!"

"Yes, honey. God has paid me a visit from heaven, and here is the answer."

In my hand was the old brown piece of cardboard, with the answer that had cost so many hours of fasting and prayer, waiting, and—yes—believing!

My wife and I sat down at the table with the list before us. As I told her the story, and we went down the list together, we both wept. There were thirteen items on the list when I came out of the closet, but I erased the last two before showing the list to my wife. These were too personal for even her to know. She has never asked me about them because she realizes it MUST remain between me and God.

The other eleven requirements make up the contents of this book. There is one entire chapter devoted to each of the eleven requirements. If you, too, have longed for the manifestations of the mighty power of God in your own life and ministry, I trust that these thoughts will inspire you. May God speak to you, as He did to me, and lead you to new victory and greater usefulness because of this book.

Since God spoke to me that day in the closet, many pages have been torn from the calendar. In fact, many calendars have been replaced by new ones. As the time has passed, I have marked the requirements from my list, one by one. The list grew smaller and smaller as I shouted the victory over Satan and marked off one after another!

Finally, I was down to the last two requirements. Satan said to me, "You've marked off eleven but here are two you'll never mark off. I've got you whipped."

But, by the grace of God, I told the devil he was a liar. If God said I could mark them all off, He would help me do it! But it was quite some time before I was able to mark off the last two.

Never will I forget the day, when I looked over my list and found there was only one thing left! Praise God, if I could mark that one off, I could claim the promise God had made to me.

I HAD to claim that promise! Millions were sick and afflicted, beyond the help of medical science. Someone MUST bring deliverance to them. God had called me to take deliverance to the people, and God has called every minister of the gospel to do the same! (see Ezekiel 34:1-4).

Many times as I traveled across the states, God poured out His Spirit on my meetings. However, I knew that when I marked the last item from my list, I would see miracles such as I had never seen before. In the meantime, I would patiently strive toward victory, trusting God to help me until the victory came. I knew that, when victory was mine, God would be glorified, and others, too, would be encouraged to seek for His power.

As I wrote this book, I was conducting a "Back to God Healing Revival" in Oakland, California. Many said it was the greatest revival in the history of Oakland. Hundreds said they had never witnessed such a dynamic moving of the power of God. Night after night the waves of divine glory swept over the congregation. Many testified of being healed while sitting in their seats. Again and again we felt the mighty power of God settling over the meeting. People rose to their feet to testify of instant healings—some of which were visibly miraculous, such as outward tumors disappearing and cripples being made whole.

I felt a goiter disappear at the touch of my hand, in Jesus' name!

There were many shouts of victory as the blind received their sight. One woman testified, "It was like coming out of the dark into the sunlight."

We prayed for a woman with throat trouble. After a few moments, she hurried to the ladies rest room. After returning to the auditorium, she testified that, after prayer, something came loose in her throat and came up into her mouth. She had hurried to the rest room to dispose of it. It was some kind of foreign growth (probably cancer), whitish-orange in color.

Ruptures, as large as a person's fist, disappeared overnight. Cancer, deafness, tumor, goiter, sugar diabetes—every known disease and many unknown—disappeared as, in the name of Jesus, we laid hands on the sick. In many cases, healings were verified by doctors' reports and x-rays.

We stood in holy awe and marvel at the miracle-working power of God. It moved, night after night, from the very beginning of this meeting. Hundreds were delivered from the power of the enemy—saved, healed, or filled with the Spirit.

In this meeting, it was impossible to have what is generally termed as a "healing line." At least 90 percent of those we laid hands on were immediately prostrated under the mighty power of God. Some danced a few steps or moved drunkenly under the power of the Spirit before falling (see Jeremiah 23:9). Under those circumstances, it was impossible to have people march on after prayer. The mighty power of God moved upon the people. It was this same power that caused John to "fall at his feet as dead" (see Revelation 1:17).

Many say that the most outstanding thing about this meeting was that such a large percentage of the sick received miraculous deliverances. It would be a conservative estimate to say that at least 90 percent—or even more—of those prayed for were marvelously healed.

One evening's service was designated "Holy Ghost Night." The building was packed to the doors, with people sitting on the altar benches. Eternity alone will reveal the number of people who were filled, or refilled, with the Spirit. We announced that, in this service, hands would be laid upon seekers for the infilling of the Spirit, according to Acts 8:17. After the sermon, all who had not already been filled during the service, came forward for prayer. With only a few exceptions, every one we touched in the name of Jesus, fell prostrate. What an unusual sight—to stand on the platform afterwards and look upon the many "slain of the Lord." They were in every available altar space and even down the aisles! Sweeter yet was the sound of the heavenly music as voices joined in united praise to God. The Holy Spirit filled obedient believers and they began to speak in new tongues and magnify God (see Mark 16:17; Acts 10:46).

Although I do not claim to possess the gift of healing, hundreds were miraculously healed in this meeting, as well as in following campaigns. I do not claim to possess a single gift of the Spirit, nor to have power to impart any gift to others, yet all the gifts of the Spirit were in operation, night after night. God confirmed His Word with signs following!

Why did I see such a change in the results of my ministry? You ask WHY? Have you not guessed?

At last the final item was marked off the list! Hallelujah! Many times, I almost gave up hope of ever being able to mark that last one off. But, at last, it was gone! By God's grace, GONE FOREVER!

With the marking off of the last requirement on

my list came the fulfillment of God's promise. The sick were healed, devils cast out, and mighty miracles were seen, in the name of Jesus, as His Word was preached!

The following chapters are dedicated to all who hunger for the MIRACLE-WORKING POWER OF GOD.

Chapter 2

THE DISCIPLE IS NOT ABOVE HIS MASTER

What strange words! Why should God speak thus to me?

Somehow, I knew I had read these words, but where? (I later discovered they were from Matthew 10:24.)   But this was the voice of God, speaking directly to ME...the same voice which spoke to Peter in Acts 10:15, saying, *What God hath cleansed, that call not thou common.* I was hearing the voice of God. All others who might share in the message of these words were, for the moment, blotted out of my mind. I had asked God for a solution to my problem and now He was giving the answer.

First of all, I needed to know that there was no *possibility* of my being above the Master, Jesus.

You say, "What is so strange about that? Surely no one would expect to be above HIM!"

But wait! You may have been seeking and expecting that very thing, just as I had. I had read God's promise in John 14:12, *He that believeth on me, the works that I do shall he do also; and greater works than these shall he do; because I go unto my Father.*   Although it hardly seemed reasonable that anyone could really do a greater miracle than Jesus, that seemed to be what the scripture said. I had wondered about the meaning of this scripture many times. The thought that a disciple could do a greater miracle than his Lord seemed to be a direct contradiction of the scripture. Now I see that this promise, like all God's promises, is true when rightly understood. *Greater works than these shall he do,* in the sense that Jesus was only one, meant He was limited by time and transportation to a small area and a few people. Those who believe on God are scattered over the face of the entire earth. Many of His modern-day disciples have circled the globe, preaching to thousands at one time by means of electrical amplification systems, and to vast unseen audiences through radio and television. Thus, they brought deliverance to greater multitudes than did Jesus. Where Jesus reached hundreds, His followers are reaching thousands. The works of power which are done today are THE SAME WORKS which He did—greater in quantity, but not in quality. Every believer has been promised the same power which Jesus used. What mighty things could be accomplished if all the followers of Jesus made use of this power!

The words quoted at the beginning of this chapter were part of the message of Christ to twelve believers. The disciples were sent out to do the very things God had called me to do—to *heal the sick, cleanse the lepers, raise the dead, cast out*

24

devils: freely ye have received, freely give (Matthew 10:8). But these wonderful promises of power also included warnings of persecution—*Ye shall be brought before governors and kings for my sake* (vs. 18). *The brother shall deliver up the brother to death, and the father the child: and the children shall rise up against their parents, and cause them to be put to death* (vs. 21). Even though Christ's followers had the same power to do the things He did, they were not promised deliverance from this persecution. Christ himself was persecuted. If His disciples could do these same works, and yet be delivered from persecution, then, indeed, the disciple would be above his master.

Yea, and all that will live godly in Christ Jesus shall suffer persecution (2 Timothy 3:12).

Persecution is one of the universal results of manifested power. Jesus was not persecuted while He remained in the carpenter shop at Nazareth. But the moment He started to do mighty things, He was called the "prince of devils," and there were many attempts to destroy His life (see Luke 4:29). The powerless religious leaders of His day feared His mighty power, and the persecution continued until He was crucified.

Peter was a "good fellow" as long as he was a mere fisherman, but when he healed the lame man, they threw him in jail (see Acts 3:7; 4:3). As long as Stephen was just a "member" in the First Church at Jerusalem, he got along nicely. But the moment he *did great wonders and miracles among the people* (Acts 6:8), he was called into judgment and stoned.

Paul never had to flee for his life because of his religion, until after he met God in a supernatural way.

I personally met very little opposition until I made up my mind to have all God had promised me as a minister.

And you will not encounter much opposition or persecution as long as you are just a "normal Christian." But when you accept God's promises for your life and begin to do the UNUSUAL, persecution will come!

This opposition may appear to come from people, but it is really directed by Satan, the commanding general of the opposing army. He uses all the methods of warfare, from direct frontal attack to "fifth-column activities."

Again and again, Jesus pointed out to His disciples the price of following in His steps, recommending that they count the cost. He offered them the opportunity to turn back if the price seemed too great in proportion to the value of the blessings. Even our master *for the joy that was set before him endured the cross, despising the shame, and is set down at the right hand of the throne of God* (Hebrews 12:2).

All who seek to share in God's power and glory must follow the same path of suffering, faithfulness, and consecration which He followed. To know the abundant, powerful life in this world and share in heaven's glory, we cannot be greater than our Master. The Son of God suffered rejection, persecution, cruel scourgings, and crucifixion at the hands of those to whom He ministered. His disciples may also suffer in order to carry the gospel of deliverance to those in bondage. *If we suffer, we shall also reign with him* (2 Timothy 2:12).

Christ himself rejected all earthly ambitions—even refusing the opportunity to rule the world (see Matthew 4:8-10). His disciple, if he is to know real power, must have the single purpose of God, rejecting all offers but His, no matter how attractive they may be. His cry, like his Masters, must be, *Lo, I come...to do thy will, O God* (Hebrews 10:7). Like Paul, he must be able to say, *I count all things but loss for the excellency of the knowledge of Christ Jesus* (Philippians 3:8).

The Son of God spent long hours alone with His Father, in order to cast out demons. He said, *This kind goeth not out but by prayer and fasting* (Matthew 17:21). So surely His disciple must also spend hours in fasting and prayer, waiting upon God and learning to think and act in unison with God, before he can expect to cast out such demons.

Men ought always to pray, and not to faint (Luke 18:1). Persistent, habitual prayer was one of the outstanding characteristics of the life of Christ.

27

When Judas desired to find Jesus in order to betray Him to the priests, he knew he would find Him in the garden of prayer. Prayer to our Lord was more important than teaching and healing. He refused to allow himself to be swept off His feet by the multitudes who *came together to hear, and to be healed by him* (Luke 5:15). He withdrew into the wilderness and prayed. Prayer was more important to Him than the working of miracles, for miracles do not generate themselves. Prayer is the cause—miracles the result. Prayer was more important to Jesus than rest and sleep. *In the morning, rising up a great while before day, he went out, and departed into a solitary place, and there prayed* (Mark 1:35). And again, *he went out into a mountain to pray, and continued all night in prayer to God* (Luke 6:12).

If the disciple could attain the same results as Jesus did without paying the same price, the disciple would be greater than his master. The "student" would have learned a better, more efficient method than that taught to him by his "teacher." In the secular world, this may sometimes happen. A musician may advance beyond the ability of the one who trained him. An artist may excel far beyond the skill of the one who taught him to draw and paint. A scientist may learn for himself things which his science teachers never knew. But the student of Jesus Christ CANNOT become greater than his teacher. He cannot learn anything Jesus does not know. He cannot find a shortcut to power with God. If he tries, he will only meet with disappointment and sorrow. His life will be shipwrecked and his ministry useless.

It is enough for the disciple [student] *that he be as his master* [teacher] (Matthew 10:25).

Chapter 3

EVERY ONE THAT IS PERFECT SHALL BE AS HIS MASTER

My spirit, which had been humbled and almost crushed by the words of the first message, was suddenly lifted up as I received the next revelation. I realized that, although I could never be above my Master, God had said I should be like my Master! (see Luke 6:40).

This is not a promise that can only be fulfilled after the coming of Christ, as some have thought. It is meant for the followers of Christ—here and now! This promise was spoken to me directly, for my own instruction and edification. But since it is a direct quotation of Scripture, it does not apply to me alone, but to every one who will believe it! It is to you! You can heal the sick! You can see miracles! You can exercise the gifts of the Spirit (see 1 Corinthians 12:8-11)! You can do the works God did! He said you could and He cannot lie!

God is not a man, that he should lie; neither the son of man, that he should repent: hath he said, and shall he not do it? or hath he spoken, and shall he not make it good? (Numbers 23:19).

My covenant will I not break, nor alter the thing that is gone out of my lips (Psalm 89:34).

31

Then, *Every one that is perfect* (who meets the requirements) *shall be as his master* (Luke 6:40). If I could meet the requirements, I could be like my Master!

Some people will say, "But that is impossible, for He was God, as well as human. And we are only human." These people disregard the clear message of these scriptures: *Verily he took not on him the nature of angels; but he took on him the seed of Abraham. Wherefore in all things it behooved him to be made like unto his brethren* (Hebrews 2:16,17).

But made himself of no reputation, and took upon him the form of a servant, and was made in the likeness of men: And being found in fashion as a man, he humbled himself (Philippians 2:7,8).

The man Christ Jesus (1 Timothy 2:5).

One night, when Jesus and His disciples were in a small boat, there came a great storm at sea, which caused the disciples to fear for their lives. Jesus rebuked the winds and sea and immediately there was a great calm. The men who were with Him in the boat marveled, saying, *What manner of man is this?* (Matthew 8:27).

This question is still the cry of many today, as they observe God's disciples—those who, by faith, are claiming His promises and going forth healing the sick, raising the dead, and ministering the Word (as Jesus himself said they should in Mark 16:17,18) with the supernatural confirmation of signs following. Many seem to think they are a peculiar and different species, or manner, of men. They are not. They are simply common, ordinary men who are full of the Holy Ghost and yielded to God as His workmen. They have discovered that they can be like their Master and have dedicated their lives to reaching that goal.

When the people at Lystra saw that Paul's command could bring healing to a man lame from his mother's womb, they said, *The gods are come down to us in the likeness of men* (Acts 14:11). Being untaught heathen, they did not know that men could have such power. Many Christian people seem to be just as unaware of the power God has made available to His people. When these poor, heathen people wanted to offer sacrifices unto Paul and Barnabas, they refused to permit this, saying, *We also are men of like passions with you, and preach unto you that ye should turn...unto the living God* (Acts 14:15).

Jesus truly was God, as well as man. Yet, as a man, He walked upon earth and performed miracles. We, as His disciples, need to ask not, "What manner of GOD is this?" but rather, "What manner of MAN is this?"

Jesus, by His own statement, was a member of the eternal triune Godhead, composed of the Father (Jehovah), the Son (Jesus Christ), and the Holy Ghost. He existed before the world was made, and shared in the work of creation (see John 1:1-3). He was not only WITH God and LIKE God—HE WAS GOD! All the attributes of deity were His. With the Father, He was omnipotent, omniscient, omnipresent, and eternal. And He is all of these today, as He sits, glorified, on the right hand of God in heaven. At the close of His earthly ministry, when He was ready to be offered as a sacrifice for our sins, He prayed, *I have glorified thee on the earth: I have finished the work which thou gavest me to do. And now, O Father, glorify thou me with thine own self with the glory which I had with thee before the world was* (John 17:4,5).

The glory was His before the world was! The glory is still His today!

But that glory was laid aside when He took on human flesh—coming as a helpless babe. He was born of a woman, circumcised like any other Jewish boy, and he increased in wisdom and stature during His childhood and growth (see Luke 2:52). He experienced every weakness and limitation of human flesh and blood. *Forasmuch then as the children are partakers of flesh and blood, he also himself likewise took part of the same* (Hebrews 2:14). He *was in all points tempted like as we are, yet without sin* (Hebrews 4:15).

He was *in the beginning with God. All things were made by him; and without him was not anything made that was made* (John 1:2,3). Yet, while He was here on earth, in the flesh, Jesus used the

34

same power that is available to every believer to-day! Such a statement would be blasphemy had Jesus himself not made it plain, again and again, that this was His plan.

Every one that is perfect shall be as his master (Luke 6:40).

As thou hast sent me into the world, even so have I also sent them into the world (John 17:18).

The works that I do shall he do also (John 14:12).

Although He was Omnipotent God, in His earthly life and ministry He declared, *The Son can do nothing of himself...I can of mine own self do nothing* (John 5:19,30). *The words that I speak unto you I speak not of myself: but the Father that dwelleth in me, he doeth the works* (John 14:10).

The answer to the disciples' question, "What manner of MAN is this?" is not found in the powers of deity which He used before He *was made flesh and dwelt among us* (John 1:14) nor in the power which is His today in the heavenlies. The answer can only be found in His earthly (human) life. He lived that life as an EXAMPLE for those whom He left to finish the work He started while He was here. *Leaving us an EXAMPLE, that ye should follow his steps* (1 Peter 2:21). He was our teacher (master) and we, His disciples (everyone that is perfect), shall be like the Master! Had He used power which was not available to us, it would be impossible for us to follow His example. But He

35

left us the promise that we would receive the same POWER, from the same Source, that was His!

Behold, I send the promise of my Father upon you: but tarry ye in the city of Jerusalem, until ye be endued with POWER from on high (Luke 24:49).

Ye shall receive POWER, after that the Holy Ghost is come upon you (Acts 1:8).

These signs shall follow them that believe; In my name shall they cast out devils; they shall speak with new tongues...they shall lay hands on the sick, and they shall recover (Mark 16:17, 18).

Behold, I give unto you POWER...over all the power of the enemy (Luke 10:19).

He that believeth on me, the works that I do shall he do also (John 14:12).

Though he was rich (in heavenly glory and divine power), *yet for your sakes he became poor, that ye through his poverty might be rich* (2 Corinthians 8:9). He folded it all away, like a garment, and laid aside His great wealth of power. *But made himself of no reputation, and took upon him the form of a servant, and was made in the likeness of men* (Phillipians 2:7). Tradition has invented the theory that He performed miracles during His childhood. But the Word of God plainly declares, *This BEGINNING of miracles did Jesus in Cana of Galilee* [where He turned water into wine] (John 2:11). He manifested no superhuman power and performed no miracles before the Holy Spirit descended upon him (see Matthew 3:16,17;

John 1:33). It was when *God anointed Jesus of Nazareth with the Holy Ghost and with power* [that He] *went about doing good, and healing all that were oppressed of the devil; for God was with him* (Acts 10:38). This was the secret of His success as a man.

What manner of man?

A man ANOINTED WITH THE HOLY GHOST AND WITH POWER. And God was with Him!

But don't forget this—Jesus was a man who was every inch a man! He faced—and conquered— EVERY TEMPTATION known to humanity! A man who could only be in one place at a time even though as God, He was omnipresent. As God, He neither slumbered nor slept (see Psalm 121:4). Yet as a man, He suffered weariness (see John 4:6) and required sleep (Matthew 8:24). He traveled from place to place on hot, weary, dusty feet—His rate of travel limited to the speed of walking. His feet, which had trod the immaculate golden streets of heaven, were soiled and bruised by the dust and stones of the filthy, unpaved oriental streets and paths of Palestine. How He welcomed the cleansing coolness of the customary foot bath before meals, when some unselfish person thought to minister to Him in this way! He suffered hunger and thirst, loneliness, weariness, and pain. The scripture says, *Every beast of the forest is mine, and the cattle upon a thousand hills...The world is mine, and the fulness thereof* (Psalm 50:10,12). Yet He claimed no part of it for himself as a man. He became poorer than the foxes and birds, for He had no place to lay His head (see Luke 9:58).

All this He did willingly for us, that we might share the riches of His glory.

When Satan came to Jesus in the wilderness (see Matthew 4:3,4), the first temptation was that He should act in the creative power of the eternal Son of God, in order to satisfy His human hunger. Had He done this, He would have been, in all points, *like unto his brethren.* It was important to the plan of Satan that this point be spoiled, if possible. But Jesus did not fall into this temptation. There was no assumption of deity in His reply. He answered firmly, as a man, *Man shall not live by bread alone, but by every word that proceedeth out of the mouth of God* (Matthew 4:4).

Jesus loved to refer to himself as the Son of man.

It is apparent by the scriptures that Jesus took upon himself our own nature and limitations, in order to be a proper example for us. It behooves us to study that example carefully, considering the question, *What manner of persons ought ye to be in all holy conversation and godliness?* (2 Peter 3:11).

Jesus was a man of power. He spoke as one having authority (see Mark 1:22). The people were astonished at this, for the religious leaders of their day knew nothing of this power. They taught traditions, theories, and theological explanations. Jesus cut across all the lines drawn by their fine points of doctrine with His words of authority! The traditional religious leaders did not speak as He spoke because they had never been given authority over the power of the enemy. How many "religious" leaders today speak as the scribes and Pharisees? Those who are LIKE their master speak with authority—the same authority Christ received from the Father while He was here on earth (see John 5:26,27). He came in the Father's name (see John 5:43) (and as His legal AGENT), to work the works of His Father. *I must work the works of him that sent me* (John 9:4). While He was on earth, Jesus chose disciples (first twelve, in Luke 9:1, then seventy others, in Luke 10:1,19) and appointed them as "deputies," giving them the same power of attorney that He had. They marveled, *Lord, even the devils are subject unto us through thy name* (Luke 10:17). They were trained under His direct supervision so they could continue *all that Jesus began both to do and teach* (Acts 1:1), when the time came for Jesus to return to the Father.

Jesus did not intend for the work He began on earth to cease when He returned to the Father. Before He went away, He left command and authority for the continuation of His work. Those who believe on Him are His agents, and are commanded to do, in His name (by His authority or power of attorney), all the things which He himself

39

would do if He were present in the body! *In my name shall they cast out devils; they shall speak with new tongues; they shall take up serpents* [not tempting God, but happening by accident, as it did to Paul, in Acts 28:3-5]; *and if they drink any deadly thing, it shall not hurt them; they shall lay hands on the sick, and they shall recover* (Mark 16:17,18). *And whatsoever ye shall ask in my name, that will I do, that the Father may be glorified in the Son* (John 14:13).

The gifts which Jesus placed in the Church, *for the perfecting of the saints, for the work of the ministry, for the edifying* [upbuilding] *of the body of Christ* [His Church] (Ephesians 4:12), cover all the great and mighty things which Jesus did while He was here in the flesh (see 1 Corinthians 12:7-11).

Jesus never taught, by inference or direct statement, that this power would be gone from the world when He went away. In His last commission to those He left behind, He declared, *All power is given unto me in heaven and in earth. Go ye therefore* [because this power is His, and through Him, ours (Luke 24:49, Acts 1:8)], *and teach all nations...teaching them to observe* [obey] *all things* [heal the sick, cleanse the lepers, raise the dead, cast out devils—freely ye have received, freely give (Matthew 10:8)] *whatsoever I have commanded you: and lo, I am with you alway, even unto the end of the world* (Matthew 28:18-20).

40

The disciples, anointed with the Holy Ghost (see Acts 2:4), *went forth, and preached every where, the Lord working WITH THEM, and confirming the word with SIGNS FOLLOWING* (Mark 16:20).

As long as men are anointed with the Holy Ghost, and God is with them, the works Jesus did will continue to be done even to *the end of the world* (Matthew 28:20).

The disciple should not be above his Master, but he shall be like his Master!

But if we are to be like Him in power, we must also be like Him in holiness, consecration, meekness, and compassion. We must be like Him in prayer and fellowship with the Father. We must be like Him in faith. We must be like Him in fasting and self-denial. If it were possible for the servant to be like Him in power without paying the price He paid, then the servant would be above his Lord.

There is a price to be paid for all that God offers to mankind. In a sense, it is all free, but there is a price of obedience and preparedness. Even our free salvation is ours only when we heed the admonition of God to repent and believe upon the Lord Jesus Christ. The "gift of the Holy Ghost" is ours only when we obey Him (see Acts 5:32). The power of God like Jesus had is for all those who meet the condition—*every one that is perfect shall be as his master* (Luke 6:40).

41

Chapter 4

BE YE THEREFORE PERFECT

These words seemed even more startling than the ones which God had already spoken. Surely this was too much! Could any mortal ever hope to be perfect? Yet, surely God would not ask me to do something which He knew I could not do! And without a doubt, this was the voice of God. I had asked bread of my heavenly Father and I knew He would not give me a stone. How thrilling to learn that this, too, was a scripture quotation, found in Matthew 5:48. It was Christ's command not only to me but to all who would be the *children of your Father which is in heaven* (vs. 45).

Perfection is the goal set by Christ for every Christian. Not every Christian has reached the goal and no Christian has the right to boast that he has attained it. Even the great Apostle Paul declared, *Not as though I had already attained, either were already perfect: but I follow after* (Phillipians 3:12). No Christian worthy of the name will be satisfied to be less than perfect. No Christian should make excuses for his imperfections, but should recognize them as failure to keep Christ's command and strive earnestly to overcome them. Perfection is the goal!

For the benefit of those who may have been taught that no person, except Christ, was ever perfect, let us note that God himself ascribes perfection to a number of men. They did not claim perfection for themselves, but God declared they were perfect.

First of all, Job, the hero of the oldest written book of the Bible was a perfect man. His friends didn't think he was perfect and they accused him of hypocrisy (see Job 8:6,13.) Satan did not think he was perfect and he accused him of serving God only because of the material blessings God had given him. Job himself was willing to admit that he was imperfect, for he declared, *I abhor myself, and repent in dust and ashes* (Job 42:6). But when Satan accused him before the Lord, God himself declared, *Hast thou considered my servant Job, that there is none like him in the earth, a perfect and an upright man?* (Job 1:8). And then, for the benefit of all who might read this scripture, God added his definition of human perfection—*one that feareth God, and escheweth* [shunneth, avoideth] *evil.*

Many object to the teaching of possible perfection on the grounds that they have never seen a perfect man. In Job's day, God declared that there was only one. Again, in Noah's day there was only one. Yet God declared that Noah was perfect! *Noah was a just man and perfect in his generations, and Noah walked with God* (Genesis 6:9).

Some declare that if one should become perfect, he would immediately be translated, as was

Enoch, but the scriptures declare that Enoch *walked with God* for at least three hundred years before he *was not* (Genesis 5:22,24), and that *before his translation he had this testimony, that he pleased God* (Hebrews 11:5).

These Old Testament saints were perfect, even before the law was given. No divinity or superhuman perfection is attributed to any of them. They were men, subject to like passions as we are, but they knew and feared God and kept His commands. They carefully avoided the overflowing evils of the idolatrous people among whom they lived in some of the most outstandingly evil ages of history.

Was perfection possible under the law?

Moses, speaking God's message to the entire congregation of Israel, declared *Thou shalt be perfect with the Lord thy God* (Deuteronomy 18:13).

Man is sometimes more critical than God. When Miriam and Aaron complained against Moses, God took his part, speaking to them out of the pillar of cloud saying, *My servant Moses...is faithful in all mine house* (Numbers 12:7). While this scripture does not use the word "perfect," surely it meets the definition given in Job 1:8.

David was not persuaded that perfection was impossible, for he declared in one of his inspired psalms, *I will behave myself wisely in a perfect way...I will walk within my house with a perfect heart* (Psalm 101:2).

All these and, no doubt, many others (such as

45

Daniel, Joseph, Abraham, Elijah, and Elisha) lived lives of holiness (perfection) without the benefit of the advantages we have been given today. God gave the complete Scriptures to His New Testament Church. *All scripture is given by inspiration of God, and is profitable...that the man of God may be perfect, throughly furnished unto all good works* (2 Timothy 3:16,17).

It was not until our own dispensation that Christ was preached, *Whom we preach, warning every man, and teaching every man in all wisdom; that we may present every man perfect in Christ Jesus* (Colossians 1:28).

To His New Testament Church, Christ *gave ...apostles...prophets...evangelists...pastors and teachers; for the perfecting of the saints, for the work of the ministry, for the edifying of the body of Christ* (Ephesians 4:11,12).

They were not given the glorious outpouring of the Holy Spirit, who is our constantly-abiding Comforter, Teacher, and Guide (see John 14:26). But He is given to us—to every one who will obey God (see Acts 5:32).

How much easier it should be for us to live perfect than for those who lived· before the Holy Spirit was given!

God says, *ye are the temple of the living God; as God hath said, I will dwell in them, and walk in them....Wherefore come out from among them, and be ye separate, saith the Lord, and touch not the unclean thing; and I will receive you, and will be a Father unto you, and ye shall be my sons and daughters, saith the Lord Almighty. Having therefore these promises, dearly beloved, let us cleanse ourselves from all filthiness of the flesh and spirit, perfecting holiness in the fear of God* (2 Corinthians 6:16-7:1).

These promises are ours and we can cleanse ourselves from all filthiness! We can perfect holiness in the fear of God! Like Job, we can fear God and shun evil and be perfect in His sight. This is not a "new thing." The doctrine of entire sanctification has been taught by many outstanding servants of Christ throughout the Church Age, and is accepted as sound doctrine by a number of major denominations. One such statement of faith is found in the Constitution of the General Council of the Assemblies of God. (Minutes and Constitution, with Bylaws, Revised (1949 edition), Page 38, Section 9.)

Entire Sanctification

"The Scriptures teach a life of holiness without which no man shall see the Lord. By the power of the Holy Ghost we are able to obey the command, 'Be ye holy, for I am Holy.' Entire sanctification is the will of God for all believers, and should be earnestly pursued by walking in obedience to God's Word. Hebrews 12:14; 1 Peter 1:15,16; 1 Thessalonians 5:23,24; 1 John 2:6."

Call it what you will—perfection, holiness, entire sanctification—it is not only possible, it is a command from God.

Be ye holy in all manner of conversation (1 Peter 1:15).

"Be ye therefore perfect" (Matthew 5:48).

You say, "I know a lot of Christians, even preachers, who say you can't be perfect and there is no use to try."

We know them, too, and they are not healing the sick or casting out demons! Sin is the devil's bridgehead in your life. Let him hold the bridgehead, if you will, but it will rob you of power!

Jesus did not allow the devil to maintain a bridgehead in his life. Just before He was crucified, He declared, *The prince of this world* [Satan)] *cometh, and hath nothing in me* (John 14:30). He had power to accomplish the work He came into the world to do because Satan had nothing in Him—not even one little bridgehead of pet sin or self-indulgence.

God's followers are admonished to keep the coasts of their lives free of Satan's bridgeheads, also. *Neither give place to the devil* (Ephesians 4:27). It is the devil's business to make you think you can't keep your life entirely free of his hideouts and landing strips. If you leave him a base of operation in your life, he can sabotage every effort you make for God and rob you of the power you need. Then the work God has given you to do will

48

go undone. You won't see the sick healed or the captives set free. Should you attempt to cast out demons, they will laugh in your face, saying, "You let us remain in your own life and then would cast us out of others!" Demons know the power of Christ and they know and fear the power of a power-filled Christian. But they have no fear of one who is not holy.

The seven sons of Sceva, a Jew and chief of the priests, decided they could say the same words as Paul, commanding demons, in Jesus' name, to come out of those who were possessed. But without the holiness and consecration of Paul, the result was not the same. *The evil spirit answered and said, Jesus I know, and Paul I know; but who are ye? And the man in whom the evil spirit was leaped on them, and overcame them...so that they fled...naked and wounded* (Acts 19:15,16). They didn't think holiness was necessary, but they found that it cannot be overlooked, if one is to exercise the miracle-working power of God! The reaction is not so immediate and violent in every case, for these "vagabond Jews" had tried it before, and only once did this happen. But *never once* did they succeed in casting out a demon. Demons only flee before the power of Christ, or of a Christ-filled life. There is no way to have power with God without holiness, for Jesus himself said, *Every one that is perfect shall be as his master* (Luke 6:40).

49

There is more that could be said about perfection. An entire book could be written in defense of the possibility of obeying the command of God, *Be ye holy; for I am holy* (1 Peter 1:16). However, enough has been said to open the eyes of those who are hungry for truth and eager to have the miracle-working power of God.

But it takes more than just knowing that holiness is possible. You must know *how* to attain it.

Not every Christian has reached the goal. Not every follower of Christ has the power that He promised. Even the twelve disciples, after performing many miracles in Jesus' name, met a demon who refused to go at their command (see Matthew 17:15,16). After Jesus had cast out the demon, the disciples asked Him why they had been unable to do it. He gave as the reason, their unbelief and lack of fasting and prayer. These twelve chosen men were, at times, found lacking in the manifestation of the fruits of the Spirit and showed evidence of such works of the flesh as pride (Mark 10:37), jealousy (Mark 10:41), and anger (Matthew 26:51). They failed to discern the plan of God and rebuked Jesus when He told them He would be killed. Jesus said to one of them, *"Get thee behind me, Satan...thou savourest not the things that be of God, but those that be of men"* (Matthew 16:23). These men had not reached perfection, but they earnestly desired to be perfect. They worked diligently to attain the promises of God, and God honored them and was not ashamed to be called their God.

Do not be discouraged because you have not attained perfection. There is an ultimate perfection which will only be reached when we see Jesus face to face at His coming. But there is a growth in grace, growing toward perfection, which must continue as long as we remain in the flesh. Our perfection may be likened to the fruit on a tree. From the time the bud appears, the apple on the inside, though very tiny, can be perfect. It has not yet taken on the size, color, or flavor it will eventually have, but in its present state it is perfect. As it is nourished, fed, and protected from frost and disease, it grows into a perfect little green apple. And as it is touched by the sunshine and rain, it finally develops into a large, beautiful, fully-ripe fruit.

It was this "unripened fruit" perfection that Paul referred to in Philippians 3:15, *Let us* [including himself] *therefore, as many as be perfect, be thus minded.* Three verses before, he had said, *Not as though I had already attained, either were already perfect* (vs. 12). Here he was speaking of the ultimate perfection of the fully-ripe fruit, the perfection which will only be complete with the resurrection of the dead. Paul didn't overlook the perfection which had already been attained, but with the true Christian spirit, he was not satisfied to

51

remain in that state. Although he didn't claim to be perfect, he declared, *I follow after...this one thing I do, forgetting those things which are behind, and reaching forth unto those things which are before, I press toward the mark* (vss. 12-14).

There is no stopping place short of ultimate perfection. Although the immature Christian may be perfect in God's sight, he will cease to be perfect when he is satisfied to stop growing! When the little green apple stops growing, it soon withers and falls from the tree. Perfection must be maintained and constantly striven after.

Growth continues by taking in food. *Desire the sincere milk of the word* [the Bible], *that ye may grow thereby* (1 Peter 2:2). An appetite for the Word of God is necessary, if we are to *grow in grace, and in the knowledge of our Lord and Saviour* (2 Peter 3:18). A real love for the Word of God is an integral part of our perfection now, as well as our ultimate perfection when Jesus comes. *All scripture is given by inspiration of God, and is profitable for doctrine, for reproof, for correction, for instruction in righteousness: that the man of God may be perfect* (2 Timothy 3:16,17).

Many folks have plenty of time to read comic strips, magazines, and novels—everything except the Word of God. They are just too busy to study the Bible! No wonder they do not grow! No wonder they have no power to heal the sick and cast out demons. No wonder they are not perfect—

52

and do not expect to be. They are not feeding their souls the proper food. *Growing in the knowledge of our Lord and Savior* comes through studying God's Word. We need to read it and believe it is God's revelation to us. It is the word of Him who cannot lie and He means exactly what he says!

Ample protection is provided for those who abide in Christ. Whatever the temptation may be, we need not sin, for *God is faithful, who will not suffer you to be tempted above that ye are able; but will with the temptation also make a way to escape, that ye may be able to bear it* (1 Corinthians 10:13).

He which hath begun a good work in you will perform it until the day of Jesus Christ (Philippians 1:6).

The Lord is faithful, who shall stablish you, and keep you from evil (2 Thessalonians 3:3).

Now unto him that is able to keep you from falling, and to present you faultless before the presence of his glory (Jude 24).

Hallelujah! It is possible to be kept by God and to live on a plane above sin.

We should not be ignorant of the devices of Satan. He can quote scriptures, too. How quickly he comes to comfort the imperfect Christian, by quoting the last half of Matthew 26:41, *The spirit indeed is willing, but the flesh is weak.* This portion should never be quoted without the first part of the verse, *Watch and pray, that ye enter not into temptation.* The entire passage indicates that we can overcome the weakness of the flesh.

Walk in the Spirit, and ye shall not fulfill the lust of the flesh (Galatians 5:16). You can be sure, Satan won't be quoting this passage of Scripture to anyone. *Now the works of the flesh are manifest...they which do such things shall not inherit the kingdom of God* (Galatians 5:19,21).

For to be carnally [fleshly] *minded is death* (Romans 8:6).

Hide behind the weakness of the flesh if you like, but don't overlook what God says will be the result! Don't accept Satan's suggestion, even when he quotes scriptures. *Resist the devil, and he will flee from you* (James 4:7).

You can be perfect! God says you can. Only Satan says you cannot.

God has provided food for you in His Word, protection for you through His Spirit, and a mighty agency for your perfecting in His Church. In order for the Church to serve this purpose, *He gave some, apostles; and some, prophets; and some, evangelists; and some, pastors and teachers; for the perfecting of the saints* (Ephesians 4:11,12).

Don't think you can attain the perfection God desires for you, if you fail to heed His warning, *Not forsaking the assembling of ourselves together, as the manner of some is* (Hebrews 10:25). Find a good church home, where God's Word is taught and believed, where the power of God is present

54

and welcome, where God is confirming His Word with signs following, and where God's people *Speak...the things which become sound doctrine* (Titus 2:1). Then make it a practice to be present whenever God and His people meet together. Only then can you be perfected by the ministry gifts which God has placed within the Church. Every service in a Spirit-filled church is planned of God to contribute something to your perfection.

Patience also plays a part in perfection. *Let patience have her perfect work, that ye may be perfect and entire, wanting nothing* (James 1:4).

The tongue also plays an important part, for *if any man offend not in word, the same is a perfect man, and able also to bridle the whole body* (James 3:2).

And above all these things put on charity, which is the bond of perfectness (Colossians 3:14).

Christ is interested in pointing out the way of perfection to you, if you desire to know it. He will place His finger on your pet sins and show you what is keeping you from the goal.

A young man once fell at the feet of Jesus and asked the question, "What must I do?" Although this young man was inquiring about the way to salvation, Jesus pointed out the way to perfection. *If thou wilt be perfect, go...* (Matthew 19:21). He laid his finger on the young man's pet sin. Like so many others, the young man felt this was too much to ask. Yet it would have been a small price to pay for perfection here and eternal life in the world to come. Jesus is just the same today. When you come inquiring how you can be perfect, He will not send you away without an answer.

Perfection and more perfection is always the Christian goal. *I press toward the mark for the prize of the high calling of God in Christ Jesus. Let us therefore, as many as be perfect, be thus minded: and if in any thing ye be otherwise minded, God shall reveal even this unto you* (Philippians 3:14,15).

As you read this book, Satan will probably whisper to you as Pharoah did to Moses, "Sacrifice in the land" (see Exodus 8:25). In other words, he tries to convince you that it isn't necessary to separate yourself from the things of the world in order to have power with God. If you persist, he will say, "All right then, but don't go too far." He infers there is danger in going too far.

You can't go too far with God. You may go too far in sin and self-righteousness. But, if you are walking in the Spirit, you need not fear going too far. No believer has gone as far as God intended, until the signs follow his ministry. We have not gone as far as we should go until we can lay hands on the sick and see them recover! No church has gone as far as the Lord intended until all nine gifts of the spirit are in operation in its services. Don't let Pharoah (Satan) keep you back! Go on! Go all the way! God's grace is sufficient for you. Don't let anything keep you from appropriating the promises of God in your own life, whether you be a lay member or a minister.

Let us go on unto PERFECTION (Hebrews 6:1).

Chapter 5

CHRIST—OUR EXAMPLE

For even hereunto were ye called: because Christ also suffered for us, leaving us an EXAMPLE, that ye should follow his steps: Who did no sin, neither was guile found in his mouth: Who, when he was reviled, reviled not again; when he suffered, he threatened not; but committed himself to him that judgeth righteously (1 Peter 2:21-23).

This scripture makes it very clear to every honest-hearted child of God that Christ is our EXAMPLE, in word and deed! We can walk as Christ walked and talk as He talked. Following His example is not a condition of the feet or lips, but of the heart! *For from within, out of the heart of men, proceed evil thoughts, adulteries, fornications, murders, thefts, covetousness, wickedness, deceit, lasciviousness, an evil eye, blasphemy, pride, foolishness: all these evil things come from within, and defile the man* (Mark 7:21-23).

For as he thinketh in his heart, so is he (Proverbs 23:7).

Before we can walk as Christ walked and talk as He talked, we must first begin to think as Christ thought! This is only possible as we "bring into captivity every thought to the obedience of Christ "

59

(see 2 Corinthians 10:5). This doesn't just happen. It is an act of determined consecration, requiring purpose and continual application, for the mind loves to wander. It also requires a willing exchange—giving up the former ways of thinking and accepting as our own the mind of Christ. *Let this mind be in you, which was also in Christ Jesus* (Philippians 2:5).

It is possible to lead a victorious thought life even though Satan tries to invade with evil suggestions. Nowhere in God's Word has He declared that man would not be tempted. Even Christ was tempted. But one can refuse to dwell upon evil things. A sane mind is a controlled mind. Evil thoughts can be driven out by filling the mind with good thoughts. Philippians 4:8 instructs us, *Finally, brethren, whatsoever things are true, whatsoever things are honest, whatsoever things are just, whatsoever things are pure, whatsoever things are lovely, whatsoever things are of good report; if there be any virtue, and if there be any praise, think on these things.* Jesus thought good thoughts. That was the reason He could walk and talk right and be a good example for us to follow.

Christ also suffered for us, leaving us an example, that ye should follow his steps, who did no sin (1 Peter 2:21,22). Christ did not live in habitual sin. He did not make excuses for sin. He resisted the devil and temptation, although He was in all points *tempted like as we are, yet without sin* (Hebrews 4:15). He is our example. And He stands ready to help us walk as He walked—in His steps!

Whosoever abideth in him sinneth not (1 John 3:6).

This is contrary to much of the religious teaching today. Multitudes of religious people today, even many who believe in divine healing, find themselves powerless when faced with those who need deliverance from sickness or demon possession. If you really want power with God, surely this matter is worthy of serious, prayerful thought, regardless of former opinions or religious teaching. There is a reason why some have power and some do not, and it is not because God is a respecter of persons. Power is a direct result of faith and faith comes by obedience.

Beloved, if our heart condemn us not, then have we confidence [faith] *toward God, and whatsoever we ask, we receive of him, because we keep his commandments, and do those things that are pleasing in his sight* (1 John 3:21,22).

Hope is available to people without holiness, but faith is not! If faith were available to people without holiness, anyone—saved or unsaved—could ask and receive anything they wanted from God, for God's unqualified promise to those who have faith is, *Whatsoever ye shall ask in prayer, believing, ye shall receive* (Matthew 21:22). But God also said, *Follow peace...and holiness,*

61

without which no man shall see the Lord (Hebrews 12:14).

Many religious teachers declare that everyone sins all the time—that it is impossible to live above sin. They say that as long as we are in this world we will sin—that we sin every day and should repent every night. But God's Word still calmly and simply states His command, *be ye holy; for I am holy* (1 Peter 1:16).

Paul, writing to the Corinthians, declared, *Awake to righteousness, and sin not; for some have not the knowledge of God: I speak this to your shame* (1 Corinthians 15:34).

People who are finding an excuse for their habitual sin, according to this verse, *have not the knowledge of God.* What a shame! It is evidence that many professed Christians are spiritually asleep. They are not led by the Spirit of God and the Word of God, for the work of the Spirit is to reprove the world of sin and of righteousness (see John 16:8). The Word, hidden in the heart, will prevent sinning against God (see Psalm 119:11).

You can't have power when you are asleep. Wake up! Quit making excuses for sin. Walk in the steps of the one *who did no sin, neither was guile found in his mouth* (1 Peter 2:22).

Jesus healed by His Word (see Matthew 8:16). *His word was with power* (Luke 4:32). The followers of Christ are assured that their words may also be words of power. We are to talk as He talked. Guile (cunning craftiness and deceit) must not be found in our mouths. Jesus walked in the Spirit and we, who are his followers, are exhorted to also walk in the Spirit (see Galatians 5:16).

Galatians 5:19-21 lists the the works of the flesh, which are *not* present in the lives of those who walk in the Spirit. *Now the works of the flesh are manifest, which are these; Adultery, fornication, uncleanness, lasciviousness, idolatry, witchcraft, hatred, variance, emulations, wrath, strife, seditions, heresies, envyings, murders, drunkenness, revellings, and such like: of the which I tell you before, as I have also told you in time past, that they which do such things shall not inherit the kingdom of God.* There are some who harbor some of these works of the flesh in their lives, making very little, if any, effort to overcome them. And yet they feel that God should honor their word and prayers and give them miracle-working power. But verse 21 says *they which do such things shall* not only fail to have power, but *shall not inherit the kingdom of God.* How could one who is not even fit for the kingdom of God expect to have power to work His works?

Using a dictionary to study this list of the works of the flesh you will find that God has listed uncleanness, lustfulness, immoderate desire, covetousness, hatred, discord, quarreling, contention, jealousy, violent anger, rage, riotous feasting, and such like. Those who do such things are *not* walking in the steps of the One *who did no sin.*

Paul exhorts us to *put off the old man* [or works of the flesh] *with his deeds...and...put on the new man, which is renewed in knowledge after the image of him that created him* (Colossians 3:9,10).

Listed below are some of the characteristics of a carnal person who is not walking in the Spirit. This list, though incomplete, may open up new channels of thought for many.

- Pride, important, independent spirit, stiffness, or precisiveness.
- Love of praise, love of being noticed, love of supremacy; drawing attention to one's self, as in conversation.
- Arguing, talkative spirit; stubborn, unteachable spirit; self-will; unyielding; headstrong disposition; driving, commanding spirit; criticizing spirit; peevishness; fretfulness; love of being coaxed and humored.
- Speaking of faults and failures of others rather than virtues of those who are perhaps more talented and appreciated than yourself.
- Lustful stirrings, unholy actions, undue affection and familiarity toward the opposite sex; wandering eyes.
- Dishonest, deceitful disposition; evading or covering the truth; leaving a better impression

of yourself than is true; exaggeration or straining the truth.

- Selfishness; love for money; love for ease; laziness.
- Formality; spiritual deadness; lack of concern for souls; dryness and indifference.
- LACKING IN THE POWER OF GOD!

If you long for God's power in your life, get on your knees and let Him talk to you about these things and give you a list of your own. God will show you the things in your life that must be changed.

A good checkup on the things we do, say, and think is to ask the question, "Would Jesus do this?" If the answer is yes, you are following His steps. If the answer is no, you are missing the mark and you cannot have God's power. You may even fail to reach heaven.

Living a life of holiness is not impossible. God commanded it and *he which hath begun a good work in you will perform it* (Philippians 1:6).

Is anything too hard for the Lord? (Genesis 18:14). God said to Paul, *"My grace is sufficient for thee"* (2 Corinthians 12:9). And His grace is sufficient for you as well.

If you really want holiness, it is not beyond your reach. And without it, you will never share in God's miracle-working power!

65

Chapter 6

SELF-DENIAL

If any man will come after me, let him DENY HIMSELF, and take up his cross daily, and follow me (Luke 9:23).

The path that Jesus walked is a way of self-denial. And if you desire to "come after him," you must DENY YOURSELF!

Someone once said, "No man spake as this man." I might add, no man ever lived like this man! And few have learned to deny self.

Mark 1:35 says of Jesus, *Rising up a great while before day, he went out, and departed into a solitary place, and there prayed.* How many who would like to do the works that He did, find little or no time for prayer? They may often pray beautifully in a crowd, or when others may be listening, but few can bear solitude, for lonely hours of the night spent in solitary prayer bring no glory to self. Self would rather find a more comfortable spot in bed and drift softly back to sleep. Self says, "I must have my rest." When asked who will pray for an hour during the night or early morning, self smiles and raises his hand. Self wants others to think well of him because he has taken this sacrificial hour of prayer. But when the hour for prayer arrives, self will turn off the alarm and go back to sleep. Self says, "It does no good to pray when you don't feel like it anyway." But Jesus says we are to deny self. This is real sacrifice and God always honors sacrifice.

In one of my early meetings in southern Missouri, good crowds had been attending for a week, but not one soul had responded to the altar calls. My wife and I decided that this MUST be changed and agreed to pray all night for souls to be saved in that meeting. We were already weary in body, for the hour was late and the service had been a hard one. Soon weariness began to overtake us, and staying awake seemed almost impossible. Again and again we had to awaken each other. There was no shouting or excitement—nothing to keep us awake except the knowledge that God had given us responsibility for the lost souls in this little community. And our desire to see them saved caused us to spend these hours in prayer. As the sun crept over the eastern horizon, we knew we had done our part and that something was going to happen in the next service. We could hardly wait!

And that night, victory came. One after another responded to the altar call, until nineteen souls had found salvation. They were shouting the praises of God, in a little country schoolhouse, under the ministry of a preacher who had only been preaching for three weeks. We went home from that service rejoicing, for God had taught us an important lesson—it pays to DENY SELF. Even when you are tired and need your rest, it pays to pray it through, whether you are stimulated by good feelings or not. Self says, "Pray if you feel like it." SELF-DENIAL says, "PRAY ANYWAY."

There are times when prayer is a delight—a time of refreshing to the weary soul. But there are other times when prayer is like meeting the enemy face to face on the battleground. We have to fight for what God says is rightly ours, dragging it by force from our adversary, the devil. There are times when we must wrestle in prayer, like Jacob, when he cried, *I will not let thee go, except thou bless me* (Genesis 32:26). There are times when the answer is slow in coming and we must hold on patiently like Daniel, who waited three full weeks (see Daniel 10:2). There are times when this wrestling may leave the body weary and the nerves overwrought, as in the case of Elijah when he prayed down the fire and rain (see 1 Kings 18-19:4). At times like that, prayer requires self-denial—but it pays. Only the person who believes in the power of prayer will deny himself the rest which his body demands, in order to pray. But God promises, *Whatsoever ye shall ask in prayer, BELIEVING, ye shall receive* (Matthew 21:22).

69

Real prayer—determined, prevailing prayer—is the greatest outlet of power on earth.

The Early Church prayed for ten days and then came the miracle of Pentecost. Moses spent forty days in the mountain talking with God, and his face shone so that he had to wear a veil. Müller prayed and, over a period of years, was able to secure one million dollars to make possible the care of 2,000 orphans.

Jesus went up on the mountain to pray and then returned to cast out demons—those which go forth only by prayer and fasting (see Mark 9:29). He did not say to the sorrowing father, "This kind goeth not out but by prayer and fasting, so wait while I go away to fast and pray." He had *already* fasted and prayed! Self-denial—fasting and prayer—was a part of His daily life. He prayed daily so that when needs arose, He was prepared to meet them.

Fasting is an important part of self-denial. The desire for food—the richest, tastiest, and best—is one of the strongest desires of self. It was for food that Esau sold his birthright. It was to physical hunger—the desire for food—that Satan directed the first in a series of temptations of Christ when He was in the wilderness. Paul, that great apostle of power, declared that he was "in fastings often" (see 2 Corinthians 11:27).

Food itself is not sinful. But if it is given undue importance, it becomes a god. And when it becomes a god, it is a sin.

70

Paul warned his church at Philippi of some whom they might be tempted to follow. He said, *They are the enemies of the cross of Christ: whose end is destruction, whose god is their belly, and whose glory is their shame, who mind earthly things* (Philippians 3:18,19).

Many who desire the miracle-working power of God in their lives are hindered because they would rather miss God's best for them than to miss a good meal.

How hard it was for me to remain on my knees in that closet of prayer, when the smell of good food cooking began to filter in through the cracks around the door! And it was not until I resolutely turned by back upon the delicious stew and went back to my closet without my dinner that I heard the voice of God. It was only then that I proved to God that He meant more to me than food.

Fasting itself has no power to accomplish miracles, unless it is done properly. The Israelites of Isaiah's day cried out, *Wherefore have we fasted, and thou seest not?* (Isaiah 58:3). God replied through His prophet, *Behold, in the day of your fast ye find pleasure, and exact all your labours. Behold ye fast for strife and debate, and to smite with the fist of wickedness: ye shall not fast as ye do this day, to make your voice to be heard on high* (Isaiah 58:3,4). Many think they are denying self, when actually their self denial is only for selfish ends—to make their voice heard on high. If our fasting is to be effective, it must be accompanied by a real heart searching and seeking after God. It must include an enlarged vision of our responsibility to be our brother's keeper. Fasting must be done unselfishly if it is to be effective. *Is not this the fast that I have chosen? to loose the bands of wickedness, to undo the heavy burdens, and to let the oppressed go free, and that ye break every yoke? Is it not to deal thy bread to the hungry, and that thou bring the poor that are cast out to thy house? when thou seest the naked, that thou cover him; and that thou hide not thyself from thine own flesh?* (Isaiah 58:6,7). When fasting is done God's way, He promises, *Then shall thy light break forth as the morning, and thine health shall spring forth speedily; and thy righteousness shall go before thee; the glory of the Lord shall be thy reward. THEN SHALT THOU CALL, AND THE LORD SHALL ANSWER: thou shalt cry, and he shall say, Here I am* (Isaiah 58:8,9).

Jesus fasted and He expects those who follow Him to fast also. But He points out that not every fast is acceptable to God (see Matthew 6:16-18). He declares that those who fast boastfully are hypocrites and their only reward is the admiration of those who look only upon the outward appearance. The fasting Jesus recommended is to be done privately—a secret transaction between the individual and God. Even the immediate family need not know that a fast is in progress. When fasting is done this way, God will hear from heaven and reward you openly by answering your prayer.

How much better for people to say, "That man has power with God. When he prays, the sick are healed, the lame walk, the dumb speak, and the blind see," than to say, "That man is surely a pious man. He fasts three days a week. He has completed a 21-day fast and is even now in the tenth day of a 40-day fast."

Some fine people have spent wasted time in sacrifice which was ineffective because they became puffed up and fasted with a spirit of boastfulness. It is Satan's business to spoil all that we try to do for God, so let us be watchful in this matter. Don't let Satan make useless, one of our most effective weapons—the weapon of self-denial through fasting.

True fasting is a matter of giving God first place over all the demands of the self-life. It goes deep into the personal life. Paul recommended that even husbands and wives (who are instructed to be considerate of each other) set aside time by mutual agreement, to give themselves to fasting and prayer. God does not condemn marriage or the rightful relationship of husband and wife. But like food, even this— which is rightfully ours—must be set aside for a time of seeking God. And it brings great profit. The closer we walk to God the greater power we have in our lives. This closeness can be achieved in only one way—*Draw nigh to God, and he will draw nigh to you* (James 4:8).

Self-denial will sometimes take you away from the company of those you enjoy. Even though they are good people and fellowship with them is great, if you want power with God, you must fellowship with Him. Fellowship with God's people is wonderful and is necessary for every Christian, especially those who are young in the Lord. But fellowship with God is more important. *Truly our fellowship is with the Father, and with his Son Jesus Christ* (1 John 1:3).

Those who have power with God—who are bringing deliverance to the sick and suffering and winning souls to Christ—are spending much time alone with God before they spend time with others.

Power does not come in a moment—it is the result of waiting upon the Lord. Self would like to hurry, but self must be denied again. Pentecost followed after ten days of waiting upon the Lord. Daniel's vision of the Last Days followed 23 days of waiting. Because Moses had not learned to wait upon the Lord to know His method as well as His will, he had to wait forty years in exile before he was ready to do the work of deliverance that God wanted him to do.

Rest in the Lord, and wait patiently for him (Psalm 37:7).

Waiting is almost a lost art. Everything today is done in a hurry, with many things requiring only the push of a button. But there is no push-button—no magic formula or "royal road"—for power with God. The man who has waited upon God commands the demons to depart, and the tormented one is free. But the man who hasn't time to "waste" in waiting speaks the same words and seems to do the same things, but nothing happens. Waiting upon God is not wasted time, although at times it may seem to you (and others) that you are accomplishing nothing. Waiting on God includes fasting, prayer, and just plain old waiting. When we pray, we talk to God. But when you have prayed until there seems to be nothing more to say, then you need to wait for an answer. Let God speak to you.

Self is restless and impatient, always clamoring for action, attention, or gratification. Self is mindful of the things of this world, the things of the flesh. But God says *If any man will come after me, let him deny himself* (Luke 9:23).

Will you come after Him? Will you do the works that He did? Then wait in His presence and let Him speak to your soul about the things of self which have not yet been denied. Let His life of self-denial be your pattern. When you do these things, you will share in His miracle-working power.

75

Chapter 7

THE CROSS

If any man will come after me, let him deny himself, and take up his cross daily, and follow me (Luke 9:23).

Very little is gained by self-denial, unless we also take up our cross and follow Jesus. By *cross*, I mean the burden of pain, sorrow, or sacrifice which we could choose to lay aside, but instead carry willingly for the sake of others. It is that which, in the natural, we *would* lay aside. But realizing there is no other way to bring salvation, deliverance, and healing to the lost, sick, and suffering, we willingly endure our cross.

Looking unto Jesus who for the joy that was set before him endured the cross, despising the shame (Hebrews 12:2). Jesus didn't have to endure the cross. On the night He was taken, He declared that He could, even at that late hour, pray to the Father and have twelve legions of angels to rescue Him from His fate (see Matthew 26:53,54). But He went to the cross because He had purposed in His heart to fulfill the Scriptures. By bearing the stripes upon His back and being sacrificed, a lamb without spot or blemish, lost and sinful

77

men were delivered from the double curse of sin and sickness.

Moses partook of this spirit when he turned away from the throne of Egypt to identify himself with his brethren—a race of slaves—that he might, through suffering and sacrifice, bring deliverance to the people (see Hebrews 11:24,26).

Obedient to the heavenly vision, Paul left his place in the Sanhedrin to join the despised and persecuted sect of Christians, that he might bring deliverance to the Gentiles. He was following Jesus and bearing his cross, when he declared, *I go bound in the spirit unto Jerusalem, not knowing the things that shall befall me there: Save that the Holy Ghost witnesseth in every city, saying that bonds and afflictions abide me. But none of these things move me, neither count I my life dear unto myself, so that I might...testify the gospel of the grace of God* (Acts 20:22-24).

When Charles G. Finney left a promising law practice to enter the ministry—an untried field for which he had no special training—he took up his cross.

However, just taking up the cross is not enough. It must be taken up DAILY! It must be taken up willingly and be carried faithfully, without fretting. It is easy to make a commitment to take up the cross during an inspiring consecration call, but many fail to take it up again the next morning, or the next.

Christ never took a vacation from His cross. The cross went with Him even on vacation! Although He stepped aside at times to rest, even then the burden was heavy upon Him.

Once when Jesus was weary and hungry, He sat down to rest by the well in Samaria, while His disciples went into the city to buy food. Yet He had the time and strength to lead a soul to salvation and to start a great revival which swept most of Samaria into the kingdom of God (see John 4).

When Jesus was confronted with one of the greatest griefs of His human life—the sudden and violent death of His cousin and dear friend, John the Baptist—He thought to slip away alone for a little time. But the people observed His going and followed Him, even then. When He looked upon them, He was filled with compassion. He put aside His own grief, took up His cross, and went forth to heal their sick and minister to their needs (see Matthew 14:13,14).

The cross was not an accident which befell Him at the end of life. He was born, and lived, and died under the shadow of the cross. He knew it was there all the time, but never once did He shun the cross. Never once did He fail to take it up daily. There was never a day that He could say, "This day is My own. I will go about My Father's business again tomorrow." There was never an experience in His life when He could say, "This is mine to enjoy. The people must wait until this is over. Then I will meet them and minister to their needs again." Even in His times of sorrow He could not say, "My own grief is so great. It is only right that I should be comforted now. Let them minister unto Me."

On the night when Jesus was betrayed, He continued to minister, knowing that the false disciple who would betray Him sat among those to whom He ministered. He rose from the table to wash the feet of His disciples, demonstrating the thing which He had said before, *The Son of man came not to be ministered unto, but to minister, and to give his life a ransom for many* (Mark 10:45).

To the eyes of the world it may seem that it was only on that dark day of Calvary that *he bearing his cross went forth* (John 19:16). But Jesus had been bearing His cross daily as He went forth, ministering among the people. He was poor, despised, lonely, and misunderstood, yet He willingly went about doing good and healing all that were oppressed of the devil so that He might bring many sons with Him into glory.

The world may not see or understand our cross, but each of us has our own God-appointed cross, whether we choose to bear it or not. It is not sickness which we are helpless to lay aside. It is not unpleasant circumstances of life which would be ours whether or not we serve God. It is that which we accept willingly—at personal sacrifice to ourselves—in order to be obedient to God and bless others.

Have you been complimenting yourself on your cross-bearing? Could it be just a matter of feeling sorry for yourself about the circumstances of your life? Or have you willingly taken upon yourself the burdens, griefs, and sorrows of others, in order to lift and bless them and bring salvation and deliverance? If you want God's miracle-working power, you must be willing to pay the price. Are you willing to take up *your* cross DAILY and follow Jesus all the way?

If you follow Christ fully, you will follow Him to the place where He was filled with the Spirit ...then on to the wilderness and hours of fasting and prayer. You will experience hours of unappreciated service and misunderstandings and persecutions. You will spend nights of watching alone in prayer. You will follow Him into the garden, bearing the burden of the lost and thinking someone nearby is sharing the load, only to find that all the rest have gone to sleep. Then you will arrive at the judgment hall for false accusations and unjust decisions. Then on to the whipping post and the cat-o-nine tails—the vinegar and the gall. You must not draw back, even from the pain and suffering of the cross.

You may say, "That sounds like losing my life altogether."

Indeed, it is. But Jesus said, *Whosoever will*

81

save his life shall lose it; but whosoever shall lose his life for my sake and the gospel's, the same shall save it (Mark 8:35).

This is life abundant—the life of POWER! It is the life of real satisfaction—knowing that your living has not been in vain! Surely it is worth every sacrifice to know that we have followed in the steps of the Son of God!

Chapter 8

I MUST DECREASE

At this point, God began dealing with me about my pride. I had never felt that I was proud. At such a suggestion—whether by preaching, direct accusation, or even the faithful dealing of the Spirit—I, like so many others, would excuse myself, calling it self-respect, poise, good breeding, or high-mindedness. But God called it SIN. *An high look, and a proud heart...is sin* (Proverbs 21:4).

In the searchlight of His presence, it was useless to make explanations. Like John of old, I was made to realize my utter dependence upon God and how little my own efforts were worth. I realized, as I had never realized before, that even my best efforts were futile and that, truly, God must take full control of my life. But before that could happen, I—my own personality, talents, knowledge, and natural ability—must *decrease* in importance in my own opinion.

I have since discovered that the power and success of any man's ministry depends upon the amount, or greatness, of God in his life. The New Testament disciples depended entirely upon *the Lord working with them, and confirming the word with signs following* (Mark 16:20). They claimed no power or holiness for themselves, although at their word of command, a man lame for forty years was instantly healed, so that he not only walked, but leaped and ran (see Acts 3:2-8 and 12-16). These were the same men who had once rejoiced, saying, *Lord, even the devils are subject unto us through thy name* (Luke 10:17). Now they have decreased in their own sight and are ready for an increased ministry. Hear them say, *Why look ye so earnestly on us, as though by our own power or holiness we had made this man to walk?...his name through faith in his name hath made this man strong* (Acts 3:12,16).

It is only as God increases in the life of one of His followers that power can increase, and this can never happen until *self* is decreased.

Oh that God's ministers—and laity as well—could realize that it is *not by might, nor by power, but by my spirit, saith the Lord of hosts* (Zechariah 4:6). The might and power spoken of here refers to man's might and power, not God's—the natural, not the supernatural.

Many great church organizations today boast of their power, influence, or popularity in their community. Their power and influence are derived from the magnificance of their great church plants, their immense bank accounts, the efficiency of their organization, their numerical strength, and their connection with the "right" people. These "right" people possess wealth and influence in this world, though many of them have never been born again by the power of God. They join the church as they would a social club. Their fine talent, soothing (spiritual sleep-producing) worship services, and beautiful forms, all help to make them popular and give them power in a world of "religious and respectable" sinners. Paul, inspired by the Holy Ghost, instructs us to separate ourselves from such folks. *Having a form of godliness, but denying the power thereof: from such turn away* (2 Timothy 3:5). These people would be greatly displeased if God should interrupt the controlled orderliness of their services by speaking through one of His prophets (as He so often did in days gone by), rebuking sin and calling them to lives of holiness and power. They make no plans, nor leave any room in their services, for the supernatural manifestation of the power of God.

True, there is a feeling of security and power in having a fine church, operating efficiently, without constant concern for financial obligations, and which is reaching multitudes with the gospel. None of these things is wrong, and we should be grateful to God for them. But all these things are nothing more than a lifeless shell if the supernatural power of the Spirit of God is not there. Such a church is a mere tower of Babel, reaching up toward a sky that is too far away. It is doomed to failure and confusion, even though it appears to be enjoying success.

What a blessing to have talent that is consecrated

and used for the glory of God. How wonderful to have knowledge. What a comfort to have appropriate accommodations. But the one thing which is absolutely necessary is the power of God.

How many fine churches in our cities find it hard to fill their auditoriums, while men and women stand in the rain outside a gospel tent pitched on the edge of town, trying to get inside? People want to see what God is doing through His ministers who have placed the power of God first in their lives— those who have been willing to decrease so that God may increase.

The *might* that Zechariah spoke of refers to the might of man, such as physical effort, natural ability, talents, forms, ceremonies, rituals, ordinances, and programs.

When the supernatural is gone, man will substitute with the natural. When the power of God is not a reality in a man's life, he will substitute songs about it, laying more and more stress upon the harmony and musical flourishes, while the real power of God decreases. Thank God for good music, but in itself it is not the power of God! The might and power of natural man will never fulfill the great commission and bring deliverance to the multitudes. Although God may use them to some extent, with the anointing of the Spirit upon them, they cannot be used as a substitute for the Spirit!

Even beautifully outlined sermons, eloquently preached by men of strong personality and charm, will never get the job done alone. For preaching is not our objective—it is merely a means to an end. If good sermonizing and beautiful preaching could get the job done, it would have been done long ago.

Oh that men would decrease and realize that without God they are nothing! If preachers could only realize that it is not altogether the beauty and forcefulness of their preaching that brings results, but the anointing of the Spirit upon the sermon, and God's *power* in the man who is preaching. People need more than to just *hear* a sermon—they need to *feel* something while it is being preached. It is the Spirit that causes people to feel the preaching.

Paul was not an ignorant and unlearned man (like some of the other disciples). He had the best education available in his time. His speech to the men of Athens, on Mars Hill, is still recognized as one of the classics of persuasive debate and of homoletical and literary arrangement (see Acts 17:22-31). His background, education, and reputation among his fellows was such that he could declare, *I might also have confidence in the flesh. If any other man thinketh that he hath whereof he might trust in the flesh, I more* (Philippians 3:4). But Paul turned it all aside and was willing to decrease. *But what things were gain to me, those I counted loss for Christ* (Philippians 3:7). Although Paul was capable of eloquent speech, he wrote to the Corinthians, *My speech and my preaching was not*

87

with enticing words of man's wisdom, but in dem-onstration of the Spirit and of power (1 Corinthians 2:4). In the next verse he tells us why he laid aside his natural talents to depend upon the power of God, and that alone. *That your faith should not stand in the wisdom of men, but in the power of God* (vs. 5).

If the power of God were given its rightful place today, more people would put their faith in God, rather than trusting in their church. There wouldn't be so many carried away by some preacher's personality, so that they are of no use to God or man unless they can work under his lead-ership.

Paul recognized the importance of the Spirit upon his preaching. *Not that we are sufficient of ourselves to think anything as of ourselves; but our sufficiency is of God; who also hath made us able ministers of the new testament; not of the letter, but of the spirit: for the letter killeth, but the spirit giveth life* (2 Corinthians 3:5,6).

People today need life and life cannot come without the Spirit. God will make us able ministers (able to bring life and deliverance) of the New Testament as we decrease all our natural ability and all that calls attention to and glorifies self.

Although Paul was a man of extraordinary knowledge, due to his fine education and his rich and varied experience, he was willing to cast it all aside, declaring that he was *determined not to know anything among you, save Christ* (1 Corinthians 2:2).

Knowledge *puffeth up* (1 Corinthians 1:8). Some people are of little use to God because they "know" too much. Paul speaks of some in the church at Corinth who are puffed up (see 1 Corinthians 4:18). By this he meant they were "over-sized," and needed to decrease, or be deflated. They seemed to be fine speakers, but Paul declared that the real test was not in their speech, but in their power. *For the kingdom of God is not in word, BUT IN POWER* (1 Corinthians 4:20).

How true this is! And how foolish we appear by trying to be something we are not, because of pride!

Pride generally takes one of five forms:

- Pride of FACE—How much better I look than those around me!
- Pride of PLACE—Don't ask *that* of one in my position!
- Pride of RACE—I come from an excellent family and must uphold the family honor at any cost!
- Pride of PACE—Everyone should be able to see that we are the most capable and efficient person available. No one else could keep up with me!

And the last and worst one of all:

- Pride of GRACE—Look at my spiritual accomplishments, how humble I am, the length of my fasts, my visions, dreams, and revelations, the gifts I possess—I must be a special favorite with God!

Whatever form our pride may take—puffing us up like a toy balloon—the first thing we must do if we are to have real power with God is to decrease—"I MUST DECREASE."

Whosoever exalteth himself shall be abased; but he that humbleth himself shall be exalted (Luke 14:11).

God resisteth the proud, but giveth grace unto the humble (James 4:6).

If you have pride in your life, the Bible says God will resist you!

How, then, can you hope for God to work with you, confirming the Word with signs following? Yes, we must decrease. Only the gold must remain. All the dross and tin must be taken away before God can work with it as He desires. And how little there is left when the dross is gone!

Chapter 9

HE MUST INCREASE

Have you ever driven across the prairie and looked at the mountains in the distance? At first sight they seem very small. But as you move closer to the mountains, you are astonished to see how rapidly they seem to grow. But the mountains really don't grow—they are still the same size as when you first saw them. The difference is that you have drawn closer to the mountains. This is exactly what happens when God "increases." God is the same, yesterday, today, and forever, and He is the same God for all men. But to some people, He seems to be a little, shriveled up, impotent God who can scarcely be expected to do anything that really matters. The problem is that these people are living too far away from Him! This is why we are instructed to *draw nigh to God* (James 4:8).

God is far away from many people because they have allowed so many other things to come in between. Some even draw nigh to God with their mouth, while their heart is far from Him (see Matthew 15:8). The only way to draw near to God is to earnestly (with all your heart) search out those things which come between you and God and get rid of them!

Pride certainly will keep God at a distance. *The proud he knoweth afar off* (Psalm 138:6). God cannot work *with* those who are far away from Him. You must come to Him humbly.

Some have excused the lack of power in their lives by saying, "The day of miracles is past. The Church is established now and doesn't need miracles anymore." Nowhere does the Scripture confirm such a thought. *Jesus Christ* [is] *the SAME, yesterday, to-day and for ever* (Hebrews 13:8).

Behold, the Lord's hand is not shortened, that it cannot save; neither his ear heavy, that it cannot hear: but your iniquities have separated between you and your God (Isaiah 59:1, 2). Don't blame God for your lack of power. Put the blame squarely where it belongs. YOU are too far from God because there are many iniquities (sins) in between.

Friends and loved ones may come between you and God. Jesus said, *He that loveth father or mother more than me is not worthy of me: and he that loveth son or daughter more than me is not worthy of me* (Matthew 10:37).

The cares of life may come between you and God, like weeds choking out a crop and making it unfruitful. Some give all their thought to the things of this life, just as though they were going to live here forever. God cannot work with such as these. To be near to the heart of God and feel the pulse beat of His compassion for the lost and the suffering, one must have a constant realization of the shortness of life and the inevitability of eternity.

Some are kept at a distance from God because of a lack of appreciation. Praise is lacking in their lives. Real appreciation for who God *is* and what He has done will bring forth praise, and praise brings us into the presence of God. *Enter into his gates with thanksgiving, and into his courts with praise* (Psalm 100:4).

God desires to be near His people so much that He sent His HOLY SPIRIT to take up abode, not just near but *within* His children. When you open your heart and allow the Spirit of God to fill you, baptize you, and take possession of every part of your body, you find that He is much nearer than ever before. He will be a much greater God to you than you have ever known. Then, as He is allowed to continue to dwell in you richly—teaching and guiding you into a closer relationship with the Father and a purer life of holiness—the greatness of God will become more and more apparent. He will *increase* in your life.

The more you come to know Him, by walking beside Him day by day, and the more you feed upon His Word, the more He will increase in your sight. All that we know of God, we know by faith. *Faith cometh by hearing, and hearing by the word of God* (Romans 10:17). So it's important to feed upon the Word of God. It is strange, but some who pay very little heed to the Word of God, still hope to have His power. But He will not honor with His presence those who dishonor His Word.

The Word will help cleanse our lives of the sins which stand between us and God. *Wherewithal shall a young man cleanse his way? by taking heed thereto according to thy word* (Psalm 119:9).

In dealing with me about this matter, God made it very plain that, if these things were allowed to persist in my life—if sin were tolerated and allowed to remain—He would continue to be at a distance from me. And at that distance, He could only be to me the little, meaningless God whom so many others professed to serve. The only way God could increase His power in my life and use me for His glory was for me to keep out everything that came between us. The only way He could remain the great "I AM" was for me to continually walk in the light of His Word and by the power of His Spirit. I had to *decrease* daily and become more absorbed in Him who must *increase.*

He MUST increase! Not *could* increase, or *might* increase—but MUST increase. There is no other choice. He must increase in control of my life if I am to have His power.

I am crucified with Christ: nevertheless I live; yet not I, but Christ liveth in me (Galatians 2:20).

"Fill me with thy spirit, till all the world
may see,
Not me, but Jesus only, shining out
through me."

94

Chapter 10

IDLE WORDS AND FOOLISH TALKING

Every idle [unprofitable] *word that men shall speak, they shall give account thereof in the day of judgment* (Matthew 12:36).

Nothing reveals the lack of real spirituality more quickly and thoroughly than foolish talking, jesting, and idle words. A perpetual flow of foolish talking and nonsensical joking labels the shallow Christian as one who has no concern for others and no burden for the lost and suffering. Although this may seem like a small matter in the eyes of many, there are few spiritual diseases which are more devastating and contagious.

God classes foolish talking along with some very unattractive companions: *But fornication, and all uncleanness, or covetousness, let it not be once named among you, as becometh saints; Neither filthiness, nor foolish talking, nor jesting, which are not convenient: but rather giving of thanks* (Ephesians 5:3,4).

Jesus himself declared, *Evil thoughts, adulteries, fornications, murders, thefts, covetousness, wickedness, deceit, lasciviousness, an evil eye, blasphemy, pride, foolishness: All these evil things come from within, and defile the man* (Mark 7:21-23). Foolishness, then, will defile a man the same as fornication! There are many who would never kill or steal, yet they will enter the pulpit and, publicly and unashamedly, reveal by their words that they are defiled within. I have never yet found a man being mightily used of the Lord to bring deliverance to the sick and sinful, whose mouth is filled with foolishness. There are those who entertain the people, getting hearty laughs in response to their jokes and nonsense. But when a real need arises, they haven't got the goods—they are unable to bring deliverance and be a blessing. At times, they may even try to put off the usual lightness and preach or teach about deeply spiritual things. But to those who hear them, there is no ring of sincerity, no real persuasion that they speak as the oracles of God. They are like sounding brass, or a tinkling cymbal.

I do not wish to infer that God's people should go around with a long face all the time, having no joy. God's people should be the happiest people in the world, for He commanded, *Rejoice evermore* (1 Thessalonians 5:16). God's people may be so happy that they will shout, sing, clap their hands, dance, laugh, and even leap for joy:

Make a JOYFUL NOISE unto the Lord, all ye lands. Serve the Lord with GLADNESS: come before his presence with SINGING (Psalm 100:1,2).

O CLAP YOUR HANDS, all ye people; SHOUT unto God with the voice of triumph (Psalm 47:1).

Let them praise his name in the DANCE: let them SING praises unto him with the TIMBREL and HARP (Psalm 149:3).

David DANCED before the Lord with all his might (2 Samuel 6:14).

Then was our mouth filled with LAUGHTER, and our tongue with SINGING: then said they among the heathen, The Lord hath done great things for us; whereof we are GLAD (Psalm 126:2,3).

Rejoice in that day, and LEAP FOR JOY (Luke 6:23).

For the joy of the Lord is your strength (Nehemiah 8:10).

The Christian who doesn't have joy is a weak Christian and is a poor representative of the faith he claims. If he doesn't begin to experience joy, he will probably soon be completely backslidden and seeking his joy somewhere else.

The joy which brings strength is rejoicing in the Lord. It is not rejoicing in the power of our own strength or wit. *But now ye rejoice in your boastings: all such rejoicing is evil* (James 4:16).

Many who are guilty of the sin of foolish, excessive, and unprofitable talking will, at first, be tempted to brand me a fanatic and rise to the defense of their pet sin. They will declare that it is a mistake to take things too seriously. However, they can find no scriptural defense for this view. Rescuing the lost and bringing deliverance to the suffering is serious business, which requires the whole heart and mind of the one who is consecrated to the task. Yet, many insist on talking in whatever manner they choose—preferring their jokes, foolish jesting, and nonsense to the power of God in their lives. If this is the way you feel, God will have to go on without you.

God chose to work through the spoken word of His representatives in this world. When Jesus was here, He said to His disciples, *The words that I speak unto you, they are spirit, and they are life* (John 6:63). What about the words you speak?

Some say that joking helps them to forget their troubles. Jesus forgot His troubles by relieving the troubles of others.

James compares the speech coming out of our mouths to water coming from a fountain (see James 3:10,11). He insists that a fountain should give forth the same kind of water all the time—not sweet water part of the time and bitter water part of the time. Then he adds, *Who is a wise man and endued with knowledge among you? let him show out of a good conversation his works with meekness of wisdom* (James 3:13).

Ephesians 4:29 says, *Let no corrupt communication proceed out of your mouth, but that which is good to the use of edifying*. Words which do not edify are idle—vain, empty, unprofitable— words. They are wasted words. God gives authority and power to the believer. This is His precious gift to us and it should not be wasted.

Jesus said, *Whosoever* [that means you!] *shall say unto this mountain, Be thou removed, and be thou cast into the sea; and shall not doubt in his heart, but shall believe that those things which he SAITH shall come to pass; he shall have whatsoever he saith* (Mark 11:23). This gives *us* the power to speak with authority, even to the extent of controlling inanimate things. It's the same power Jesus used when He spoke to the wind and the sea and calmed the storm (see Mark 4:39). It's the same power Moses used when he spoke to the rock in the desert and water gushed forth (see Numbers 20:8). Joshua used the same power when he commanded the sun and the moon to stand still (see Joshua 10:12,13). Jesus demonstrated this power when He spoke to the fig tree, saying, *No man eat fruit of thee hereafter forever* (Mark 11:14). He commanded the tree to die and it died! It was on this occasion that He expressly delegated this same power and authority to any who believe.

Men and women who have God's power in their words can speak deliverance from every oppression of Satan—words that bring salvation for the soul and healing for the body. To them—His representatives—Jesus warned that idle, wasted words would be brought into judgment. Words which could have been life, deliverance, and bread to starving souls, but instead were words of chaff!

99

In a world of dying, starving souls and suffering humanity, how sad it is to withhold the one source of life and deliverance, and offer stones for bread! Instead of being a fountain which gives forth the pure water of life, too many give forth a stream of froth and foolishness which, if not poisonous, is utterly unattractive and unprofitable! How will we measure up in that day, when our deeds and *words* are judged by the standard of the Word of God: *If any man speak, let him speak as the oracles* [utterance or speech] *of God* (1 Peter 4:11).

Those who insist on continuing in their foolishness are like a group of young ladies who were seen in a vision by a consecrated saint of God. They were too busy making daisy chains to warn the passersby that their steps were leading to impending danger. Just ahead was an awful precipice, where they could quickly fall and be dashed to death on the rocks below. This kind of selfish preoccupation is far from the spirit of Christ, who had compassion upon the multitudes.

I do not mean to infer that there is no place for humor in the conversation of the Christian—or even in the preaching of the Word. Many times, our speech or preaching can be humorous and still be sanctified. A bit of humor, especially when used to illustrate a point, can be very profitable. It arouses the attention and interest of the hearers and drives home the message of the gospel, so that souls turn to God. Used in this manner, it is not idle and unprofitable.

The reason some Christians speak so many idle words is simply because they speak *so many words!* They talk so much that they have no time to think or listen to the voice of God. Foolish words come so easily—we don't even have to think about them. We hear foolish words everywhere—they seem to be produced by repetition. The spirit of the age is an ever-increasing spirit of levity, which makes serious thinking difficult for both sinner and saint. It is typified by the oft-repeated phrase, "Don't take life too seriously. After all, you'll never get out of it alive." In such an age, it takes real effort and consecration to *study to be quiet* (1 Thessalonians 4:11) and wait before God till we receive His powerful words. But the wise man will do it, for *he that hath knowledge spareth his words* (Proverbs 17:27), *but the mouth of fools feedeth on foolishness* (Proverbs 15:14). *In the multitude of words there wanteth not sin* (Proverbs 10:19). *A fool's voice is known BY MULTITUDE OF WORDS* (Ecclesiates 5:3).

As I mentioned in previous chapters, holiness is necessary if we are to have God's power in our lives. And holiness is not complete until it has taken possession of the tongue. *But as he which hath called you is holy, so be ye holy in all manner of conversation* (1 Peter 1:15).

I beseech you, brethren, to give this matter

your prayerful consideration. Many who are lost and suffering will never find deliverance unless you make yourself ready and take them the delivering power of Jesus Christ. Consecrate yourself to God afresh and present your body to Him, a living sacrifice. Do not forget or neglect to include your *tongue, your lips, and your voice!*

Let your speech be alway with grace, seasoned with salt (Colossians 4:6). *Keep that which is committed to thy trust* [the power to speak in God's stead, and bring deliverance], *avoiding profane* [not holy] *and vain* [empty, worthless] *babblings* (1 Timothy 6:20).

It is my prayer that all who read this book will cast aside *all* things which hinder the freedom of power of God in their lives. Put your all on the altar and carry a burden for the lost and suffering. Remember, God can go on without you, but if *you* go on with God, you must go His way. Put foolishness aside *now*! Get out of the "eddy" and into the stream of God's power.

God's promises are for you if you will only believe them, meet His conditions, and *pay the price.*

Chapter 11

PRESENT YOUR BODY

I beseech you therefore, brethren, by the mercies of God, that ye present your bodies a living sacrifice, holy, acceptable unto God, which is your reasonable service (Romans 12:1).

God doesn't make a habit of using that which does not belong to Him. He uses vessels which are yielded to him—consecrated, sanctified, set apart for His use. Do you want God to use you? Then you must present your body to Him. It must be completely yielded and surrendered to God. A body that is not completely yielded and surrendered to God is still, more or less, domineered by Satan or self.

At special times, many present their bodies to the Lord for His use in extending the borders of His kingdom. But it is obvious, since they are not being used, that many who have presented themselves have not been accepted.

God does not refuse them because He has no need for laborers. Christ himself gave us the command to pray that more laborers would be sent forth because *the harvest truly is plenteous, but the laborers are few* (Matthew 9:37).

God does not refuse them because of their

handicaps, for He often uses those who seem to have few natural qualifications. Peter and John, men greatly used of God, were *unlearned and ignorant men* (Acts 4:13). Moses was "slow of speech." *Not many wise men after the flesh...not many noble, are called; but God hath chosen the foolish things of the world to confound the wise; and God hath chosen the weak things of the world to confound the things which are mighty; And the base things of the world, and things which are despised* (1 Corinthians 1:26,27,28). Do you think you are handicapped? Almost everyone is handicapped in some way.

A young man, grateful for his salvation, wanted to share his testimony in a street meeting so others might know the matchless grace of God. But he was unable to give his testimony because of a stammering problem. Yet his love for God and his desire to witness for Him drove him to his knees to seek God's help. God heard his cry and delivered him. He became a great preacher of the gospel and, for many years, was the chief speaker at a large camp meeting in New York.

To be an acceptable sacrifice before God, your body need not be strong or beautiful. David Brainard, a great missionary to the American Indians, was told that he was dying of Tuberculosis. He was told that total bed rest was necessary if he was to live for more than a few weeks. But he brought what he had to God and made an acceptable sacrifice. He fell on his face, crying, "Give me souls or take my soul!" Then he rose up and went out to minister among the people God had laid upon his heart. Thousands of souls were won to Christ through his years of ministry.

The only reason God refuses some is because *they are not acceptable*! God makes only two requirements for an "acceptable sacrifice"—it must be *holy* and it must be *His*.

That which is not holy is an abomination to God. A sacrifice which is defiled by the habits and sins of the world is no more acceptable to God than the pig which was offered upon the sacred altar of the Temple at Jerusalem by Antiochus Epiphanes. Such a sacrifice will not be accepted.

That which is God's must be His not only on Sunday and prayer meeting night, but seven days and nights *every week*. And it must be presented with no strings attached, with a heart that cries, "I renounce all authority over this gift, now and forever. It is Yours to use, to set aside, or to destroy. Whatever You choose to do with it, it is Yours. If it is only a hidden ministry of prayer and personal testimony—I say yes, Lord. If it is a ministry in my own hometown, that is all right. If it takes me far across the sea to strange lands and unfriendly people...if it requires that I die for my faith at the hands of persecutors...if I must live under conditions that are worse than death...still, this body is Yours. Do with it as You please—feed it or starve it...chill it in the far North or let it suffer in the heat of Africa...exalt it or humiliate it...it is all Yours."

Acceptable consecration is like handing God a blank paper with your name signed at the bottom, which says, "Fill it in any way You want and it shall be my contract for the use of my entire life."

A sacrifice is not complete by merely saying yes to specific callings or requests of the spirit of God when they are given. Total sacrifice involves a wholehearted determination to devote your entire life to doing the will of God, no matter what it is or what it may cost. It is the realization that *Ye are not your own* (1 Corinthians 6:19).

You may find a small measure of power and a small measure of blessing, when you have made a small measure of sacrifice. But if you would really experience the free flow of God's miracle-working power in your life, you *must* present your body, a living sacrifice, holy and acceptable unto God.

Chapter 12

A PARTAKER OF HIS DIVINE NATURE

Whereby are given unto us exceeding great and precious promises: that by these ye might be PARTAKERS OF THE DIVINE NATURE (2 Peter 1:4).

God IS power. There is nothing good in this world except that which comes through the power of God. When He came into this world in the flesh, Jesus himself declared that He derived His power from God. *I do nothing of myself* (John 8:28). *The Son can do nothing of himself* (John 5:19). *I am in the Father, and the Father in me. The words that I speak unto you, I speak not of myself: but the Father that dwelleth in me, he doeth the works* (John 14:10).

After making this emphatic statement in John 14:10, Christ turned to His disciples with a promise, *Verily, verily, I say unto you, He that believeth on me, the works that I do shall he do also; and greater works than these shall he do; because I go unto my Father* (John 14:12). But, just as His own work and fruitfulness was conditional on His abiding in the Father, so our work and fruitfulness is conditional on our abiding in Him. *Abide in me, and I in you. As the branch cannot bear fruit of itself, except it abide in the vine; no more can ye, except ye abide in me* (John 15:4). *Without me ye can do nothing* (John 15:5).

The branch is *partaker* of the nature of the vine. The same sap flows through it. The texture of the wood is the same. The leaves are the same. The fruit is the same. The bark is the same. It is a part of the vine! As long as it remains in the vine, it can do whatever the vine does. But whenever it is separated (cut off) from the vine, it can no longer do what the vine does. The life-giving sap ceases to flow through the branch and it is no longer partaker of the nature of the vine. For it is the nature of the vine to bring forth fruit, and the severed branch can never do that.

Branches can be cut off and they can also be grafted.

We, as sinners saved by grace, are compared in God's Word to the branches of a wild olive tree which were grafted in. Having been grafted in, we become partakers *of the root and fatness of the olive tree* (Romans 11:17). If a graft is done well, made so that nothing interferes with the flow of the sap into the new limb, it will soon begin to look and act like the other parts of the tree.

What a privilege to be made a partaker of the divine nature of God—to *look* so much like Him that others will realize that we have been with

Jesus...and to *act* so much like Him that we also do the works that He did!

We can only be partakers of this divine nature because of His promises—through faith in His promises. We partake of the divine nature, in its effectiveness, as we exercise the gifts of the Spirit and, in its essence, as we show forth the fruits of the Spirit. It is in the exercising of the gifts of the Spirit that God shows forth, through us, His miracle-working power. *Having then gifts differing...whether prophecy, let us prophesy according to the proportion of faith* (Romans 12:6). This is the secret of our accomplishments for God. They are done according to the proportion of faith. We are partakers of the divine nature according to the proportion of faith. With little faith, the branch is barely alive—the sap barely gets through, creating a few green leaves that give hope that fruit *might* come. With more faith there is more of the divine nature—fruitfulness. With much faith, there is *abundant life*—the life-giving sap flows freely to every part of the branch, and the weight of the fruit almost bows it to the ground!

He who is a partaker of the divine nature of Christ will also be a partaker of His nature of meekness and humility. The love and compassion of the nature of Christ will be apparent in all the activities and contacts of his daily life. The gentleness, kindness, goodness, longsuffering, peace, joy in service, self-denial (temperance)—all these will be part of the life of the person who is a partaker of the divine nature of Christ. These may not have been part of your nature before Christ came to dwell in you, but when you become a partaker of His nature, they will replace the things of your own carnal nature.

Then when you are a partaker of His divine nature, you will have wisdom that comes from following the leading of the Spirit. It is not the wisdom which is purely natural, or gained merely from observation, but is a Spirit-led wisdom which is incomprehensible to those who do not understand the leading of the Spirit. Knowledge will come to your mind out of the knowledge stored in the mind of God. Things which you need to know, but have no other way of knowing, God himself will reveal to you. There will be power, for God is power! And miracles and signs will follow. The sick will be healed—the lame will walk and cancers will vanish at your command. The blind will see and the deaf will hear. When necessary, even the secrets of people's hearts will be made manifest. Souls will be stirred from the sleep of spiritual death and be brought again from the dead into the will of God.

God plays no favorites. The price of power stands—it's the same for all. And the same power is available to all who will pay the price! It is for everyone who will take, by faith, the "exceeding great and precious promises" for himself, believing with all his heart that God meant exactly what He said. It is then that we become a *partaker of His divine nature*, and the door opens to new adventures of faith, beyond your wildest dreams!

Chapter 13

PERSONAL THINGS

These are the eleven points that God revealed to me. As I have shared them with you, I trust that God has used them to bring you closer to himself, into a position to receive His miracle-working power in your own life.

You may be wondering what those last two personal things were which God showed me. I cannot tell you for, deep in my heart, I do not feel the Lord would have me do so. But this chapter deals with the matter of "personal things." And as you consider the message of this book, read the Bible, and wait before the Lord in prayer, I am sure that you, too, will find some "personal things" which require attention.

I pray that you may have been inspired to *press toward the mark for the prize of the high calling of God in Christ Jesus* (Philippians 3:14), and to keep pressing on until God is working in your life with miracle-working power. Strive earnestly for perfection in the sight of God and seek to be in His perfect will. *Let us therefore, as many as be perfect, be thus minded; and if in anything ye be otherwise minded, God shall reveal even this unto you* (Philippians 3:15).

This is God's promise—He will reveal what you need to know about *your* life. You have no need to know about the personal, pet sins which God pointed out to me. But you do need to recognize your own pet sins, those which keep you from having the power God wants you to have!

In my experience as an evangelist and pastor, I have found that most people have a pet sin which they have pampered, petted, and developed for years. Paul terms it *the sin which doth so easily beset us* (Hebrews 12:1), or your "besetting sin." He also says it must be *laid aside* if we are to gain the prize at the end of the race. *Let us lay aside every weight, and the sin which doth so easily beset us, and let us run with patience the race that is set before us* (Hebrews 12:1).

Many good people could have been effective Christian workers had they not dropped out of the race. But they became so discouraged by the excess weight of things they refused to lay aside that they gave up and became skeptics. They question the power which God promised to the believer "with signs following"—the works which Christ did. Many, across the land today, are on the verge of giving up all hope of ever knowing God in the fullness of His power. DO NOT GIVE UP. Get alone with God. Whatever the cost may be, seek Him earnestly, until He has shown you the things that must be cleansed from your life before you can experience His power.

114

A rich young ruler once came to Jesus, anxious to know what was wrong with his religious experience. He was so anxious to know that he literally came running and fell down at the Master's feet. When he inquired, "What must I do?" Jesus replied, "One thing thou lackest." Then Christ put His finger on the young man's pet sin and instructed him on how to get rid of it (see Mark 10:21). As you seek the Lord, remember that He is always faithful. He will reveal your pet sin to you, just as He revealed the sin of the rich young ruler to him. Failure to place your sin upon the altar will cause you to "go away grieved," just like the rich young ruler. When God speaks to you—no matter how small the voice—OBEY! Get rid of that pet sin and go on with God!

Your pet sin is:

- the sin you don't want the preacher to preach about
- the sin you are always ready to defend—for which you are always ready to make excuses
- the sin which, although you do not admit it is sin, you prefer to do when you think no one will find out
- the sin which most easily holds you captive
- the sin which causes clouds of doubt and remorse to cross your spiritual sky just when you really feel the need to contact God

- the sin which you are most unwilling to give up
- the sin which you think is so small that God should scarcely be able to see it, and yet so large that you are sure you could never live without it (the sin which must be FLUNG [Weymouth] aside or else you must drop out of the race.)
- the sin you continually try to make yourself believe is an "infirmity."

Be honest with yourself. Recognize your sin and call it SIN! Do not call jealously "watchfulness." If you are covetous, don't call yourself economical. If you are guilty of the sin of pride, don't dress it up as self-respect. If you are one of those who constantly exaggerates (stretches the truth), you may as well admit that all which is not the truth is a lie! Are you bound by a perverse (stubbornly wrong) demon? Be careful, or you will pride yourself on just being very firm. If your besetting sin is lust, don't excuse it by saying you are just oversexed by nature. Don't call criticizing the gift of discernment, or claim to be a good judge of human nature.

Are you fretful and complaining? Satan will tell you that you are nervous and that, in your condition, this fretfulness can't be helped. Come on, friend. Be honest with yourself and God. Call it exactly what it is. If it is sin, call it sin. Then get

116

down before God and ask Him to set you free and make you an overcomer.

No doubt, many excuse their "little" sins by pointing out, "Why, everyone does that!" Remember, you can't pattern your life after other people's mistakes. How do you know that God hasn't spoken to them many times about this very thing? Don't join them in their disobedience. And what if God hasn't spoken to them about it? Remember the exhortation of Jesus to Peter, when he inquired about what would be required of another disciple, *What is that to thee? follow thou me* (John 21:22).

Consecration has much to do with personal things. It is the putting off—putting out of our lives—of the hundred and one "little things" that, in themselves, may not be sin, but which, if allowed to remain, take the place that Christ should have. For example, many professing Christians admit that they do not read their Bible as much as they should. They say they are so busy that they just don't have time to read it. Yet these same people have time to read all the daily and Sunday comic strips, various magazines, and stories in other publications. There is but one logical conclusion— these comics, magazines, and other stories are more important to them than the Word of God. Some of this reading might be of a rather harmless nature and not actually sinful in itself, *except* for the fact that it has crowded Christ out of His rightful place in the life of the reader. Thousands who profess to

117

be believers in the Lord Jesus Christ today would have more power in their lives if the time they spent listening to ball games, "soap operas," and "perpetual emotion dramas" was spent alone in the closet of prayer, listening to the voice of God. These are some of the "little foxes that spoil the vine," destroying the tender grapes and robbing God's people of fruitfulness.

Many would have more power in their lives, if the time they spent in front of their television sets watching wrestling matches was spent on their knees, wrestling against Satan and the principalities and powers and *the rulers of darkness of this world*, and *against spiritual wickedness in high places* (Ephesians 6:12).

It isn't always the harsh, gross sins that stand between man and God. In fact, the sins which seem to keep most people from the best God has for them are the things that "everybody does." But I'd be careful about saying "everybody does it." Those who are carrying a burden for this lost, sin-sick, Christ-rejecting, hell-bound world, and who are doing the works which Christ promised they would do, with signs following their ministry, and who are bringing deliverance to the needy, have long ago laid those things aside. You may be right in saying, "*nearly* everyone in my church does it." But don't forget that, while they are doing these things, they are wondering why they don't have the miracle-working power of God and the gifts of the Spirit operating in their lives. Many of them probably wonder if they are ready for the Rapture!

Many times, after preaching on the coming of the Lord, I have made altar calls for those who are not sure they are ready. I have often been surprised at the great number of people who professed to be saved and filled with the Spirit who raised their hands! If these so-called saints are not living a sufficiently victorious life so as to be assured that they are ready for the Rapture, they cannot have consistent miracle-working power! They may have a prayer answered now and then, but the times in which we live demand more than that. You cannot pattern your life after the crowd. There is only one whose life is worthy to be a pattern for ours, and that one is JESUS.

Some may not be willing to accept the teachings of holiness found in this book. But I make no apology. I have quoted Jesus all through the book, and if you disagree with Him, it is time to reconsider and begin agreeing with God. *Can two walk together, except they be agreed* (Amos 3:3). If you expect to walk with God and have power in your life to work the works of God, it is time to agree with God. When you fully agree with God, you may be in disagreement with some others whose opinions you honor and value, but it is better to agree with God.

At some point in life, every person reaches the fork in the road and must decide which direction he will take. Throughout the ages, men of God have chosen the way that seemed hard and brought persecution, suffering...and POWER. Others have chosen the way that seemed more attractive, and led to prosperity, popularity...and destruction. Picture Lot of old, as he pondered the best course to take. There was the watered valley, with the prosperous city of Sodom at its center. Surely this was an easier way than to turn to the lonely, rough hills. He felt sure he could go among those people in the valley, mind his own affairs, and not partake of their sins. And even at the end, God still counted him as a "righteous man." But Lot didn't have the power of God in his life. He couldn't even rescue his own married daughters from the destruction of Sodom, for he seemed to them as one that mocked (see Genesis 19:14).

This popular but destructive way is still open to those who choose it. But, thank God, there is a better way and it is open too. It is marked by the footsteps of such men as Moses, who *by faith...when he was come to years, refused to be called the son of Pharoah's daughter; choosing rather to suffer affliction with the people of God, than to enjoy the pleasures of sin for a season* (Hebrews 11:24,25).

Joseph also chose God's way, keeping himself pure, even though it meant spending years in an oriental dungeon, with no assurance (except in his soul) that he would ever be released.

As a slave boy, Daniel declined to drink the

king's wine. Choosing to travel God's road meant a trip to the lion's den for Daniel, but at the end he kept his appointment with God.

These men said *no* to Satan so they could say *yes* to God. Moses weighed the pleasures and treasures of Egypt against the call of God and decided in favor of the call of God. He knew the pleasures of sin could only last for a season. He esteemed *the reproach of Christ GREATER RICHES* (Hebrews 11:26). Moses had a true sense of values which many today do not have. They seem to think greater riches are found in Egypt—Hollywood, Broadway, or Wall Street. But in order to say yes to God, we first must say no to the things of the world.

Those whose minds were set upon worldly things would have quickly advised Moses that he was making a very unwise choice, giving up so much for so little. But Moses received his reward— He was a friend of God and talked with Him face to face. His face shone so bright with the glory of God that people could not bear to look upon it. And, working hand in hand with God, he led three million people out of bondage into liberty. He saw them miraculously delivered time after time as they were kept by the hand of God so that *there was not one feeble person in all their tribes* (Psalm 105:37). Truly, this is the reward which we seek today—that we might be able to bring salvation and deliverance to needy people. God still gives that reward to those who hear His voice and obey His call—to those who say no to the world and yes to God!

In days gone by, God *sought for a man...that should make up the hedge, and stand in the gap before* [him] *for the land that* [He] *might not destroy it* (Ezekiel 22:30). God is still looking for such men today. God's holiness demands that He send judgment upon a wicked world. The presence of righteous people in the world is all that holds back the floods of God's judgment. Moses stood in the gap for the Children of Israel and their lives were spared (see Exodus 32:10,11). Abraham stood in the gap for Lot and his family, when they were in Sodom. And if Lot could have gathered a group of righteous people, saved from their sinfulness through his testimony and influence, he could have stood in the gap for the entire city of Sodom (see Genesis 18:23; 19:15).

Our generation today is a wicked generation, similar to that of Lot's day. It is a sin-sick, judgment-bound generation. The wrath of God has already been pronounced against *all* who partake of the wickedness of the world. But God does not take pleasure in pouring out judgment. Now, as in days gone by, He looks for a man—any man or woman—who is willing to stand in the gap. He looks for someone who loves people enough to make the sacrifices necessary to hold back the storm of judgment—someone who will stand, with the storm beating upon his back, and raise his voice long and loud, pleading with the people to flee from the wrath to come.

The stage is set for the last great scene of the great story, "The History of Man upon the Earth." Soon the curtain will rise on that last scene—the terrible Tribulation Period. Then, after the righteous have been snatched away, the wrath of God will be poured out without measure upon this wicked world. The clouds are gathering, the lightning is flashing, and the thunder rolls—gusts of the winds which precede the storm can be felt with ever-increasing frequency and force.

Lift up your eyes, and look on the fields; for they are white already to harvest (John 4:35). It is more urgent than ever before that the servants of God place the work of the harvest ahead of everything else. They must work, for *the night cometh, when no man can work* (John 9:4). It is time to use *all* the power that God provided to save as much of the precious harvest as possible before the storm breaks. It is time for you and me to faithfully stand in the gap where God needs us.

How sad, when God sought hopefully, for a man to stand in the gap, but had to say, *I found none. Therefore have I poured out mine indignation upon them; I have consumed them with the fire of my wrath* (Ezekiel 22:30,31).

God is still looking for men to stand in the gap! He is still looking for laborers for the harvest. He offers the same wages and rewards for those who serve in this last hour, as for those who have stood the heat of the battle before us. All He asks is that we respond to His call and faithfully carry it out. Will you say *yes* to the call of God? Will you give Him your *all*? Will you accept His best—the miracle-working, soul-saving power of God—which brings deliverance to the lost and to the sick and suffering?

Much has been done for the deliverance of humanity by holy men and women of God, from the time of righteous Abel until now. But as I look into God's Word and behold the mighty promises of God, I find that miracles were wrought when someone dared to believe. I am persuaded that it remains to be seen what God can do with a man or woman who is willing to go all the way with Him and never doubt in his heart! What immense power could be turned loose against the enemy who is destroying mankind, if a great army of men and women would all stand together upon God's promises and believe for His miracle-working power!

YOU can be that *one*—or *one* of that great army!

When God looks for a man, will you volunteer? WILL YOU BE THAT MAN?

124

Other Materials
By
POWER PUBLICATIONS

Books

By R.W. Schambach

You're One In A Million
Power For Victorious Christian Living
Four Lambs
Miracles: Eyewitness To The Miraculous
You Can't Beat God Givin'
What To Do When Trouble Comes
I Shall Not Want
The Secret Place
After The Fire
When You Wonder "Why?"
Power Of Faith For Today's Christian
Triumphant Faith
Power Struggle: Faith For Difficult Relationships
The R.W. Schambach Collection

By Donna Schambach

Tell, Teach & Train

By A.A. Allen

God's Guarantee To Heal You
The Price Of God's Miracle Working Power
Demon Possession Today And How To Be Free

Videos

By R.W. Schambach

Fabulous Fakes: *A Religion Of Form Vs. A Religion of Force*
Miracles
The Army Of The Lord
How To Raise The Dead
A Life Of Faith
Turn Up The Heat
Don't Touch That Dial
Break The Back Of Debt
Campmeeting With R.W. Schambach

Cassettes

By R.W. Schambach

(2) Tape Series
Fabulous Fakes: *A Religion Of Form Vs. A Religion of Force*
The Violent Take It By Force
Power Struggle
After The Fire
Shout

(4) Tape Series
Four Freedoms
A Little Bit Of The Bronx
Fear Not
Classics Of The Faith: *Classic Sermons On Faith & Power*

(6) Tape Series
When You Wonder "Why?"
The Tent Masters

(10) Tape Series
R.W. Schambach's Classic Sermons

By Donna Schambach

(2) Tape Series
How Does Healing Come?
The Dream Team

(3) Tape Series
Revival NOW

For more information about this ministry
and a free product catalog, please write:

SCHAMBACH REVIVALS, INC.
P O BOX 9009
TYLER, TX 75711

To order materials by phone, call:
(903)894-6141

WHEN YOU NEED
PRAYER

Call the Power Phone

Every day of the week, 24 hours a day, a dedicated, faith-filled, Bible-believing prayer partner is ready to talk with you and pray about your needs. When you need prayer call:

(903)894-6141

If during the reading of this book, you made a decision to follow Christ, R.W. Schambach has a special gift for you. He has written a booklet that will help you continue growing in your new walk with God. It is called, *"You're One In a Million."* And, by simply writing or calling the ministry of Schambach Revivals and letting us know of your decision, we will mail this booklet to you, free of charge. Write or call:

Schambach Revivals
PO Box 9009
Tyler, TX 75711
(903) 894-6141